Melvyn Matthews is Canon Er
had responsibility for the cathe
spirituality. He also oversaw th
visitors the cathedral receives. ... some time, he was the Senior
Chaplain to Bristol University but, before that, taught in the
Department of Theology and Religious Studies in the University
of Nairobi. More recently, Canon Matthews was the Director of
Ammerdown Centre, an ecumenical laity centre near Bath. He has
written a number of books, the most recent being *Rediscovering
Holiness: The Search for the Sacred, Both Alike to Thee: The Retrieval
of the Mystical Way* and *Nearer than Breathing: Biblical Reflections on
God's Involvement in Us* (published by SPCK). He is married with
children and grandchildren, and enjoys sailing.

LIT BY THE LIGHT OF GOD

Prayers and Meditations through the Year

Melvyn Matthews

SPCK

First published in Great Britain in 2005

Society for Promoting Christian Knowledge
36 Causton Street
London SW1P 4ST

Copyright © Melvyn Matthews 2005

All rights reserved. No part of this book may be reproduced or
transmitted in any form or by any means, electronic or mechanical,
including photocopying, recording, or by any information storage and
retrieval system, without permission in writing from the publisher.

SPCK does not necessarily endorse the individual views contained in its
publications.

*Every effort has been made to acknowledge fully the sources of material
reproduced in this book. The publisher apologizes for any omissions that
may remain and, if notified, will ensure that full acknowledgements are
made in a subsequent edition.*

Scriptural quotations are taken from the New Revised Standard Version
of the Bible, copyright © 1989 by the Division of Christian Education of
the National Council of the Churches of Christ in the USA. Used by
permission. All rights reserved.

British Library Cataloguing-in-Publication Data
A catalogue record for this book is available from the British Library.

ISBN 0–281–05642–0

1 3 5 7 9 10 8 6 4 2

Typeset by Graphicraft Ltd., Hong Kong
Printed in Great Britain by Ashford Colour Press

Contents

PRAYERS FOR PENTECOST

OTHER PRAYERS

Contents

TWO EVENING PRAYERS

THE FINAL ARRIVAL

Acknowledgements

I am grateful to the following authors and publishers for permission to reproduce copyright material:

Stephen Orchard

The Very Revd Hugh Dickinson: A prayer from *Heart in Pilgrimage: Prayers in Salisbury Cathedral*, published and produced for the Dean and Chapter of Salisbury Cathedral by R. J. L. Smith & Associates, 1996

Women's World Day of Prayer: Two prayers by Palestinian women of Jerusalem from the 'Women's World Day of Prayer Order of Service', 1994

L'Osservatore Romano: Prayer by Ecumenical Patriarch Bartholomew of the Orthodox Church

Ateliers et Presses de Taizé, 71250 Taizé-Communauté, France: Two texts by Br Roger of Taizé

Random House Group: Extracts from Etty Hillesum: *An Interrupted Life and Letters from Westerbork: The Diaries, 1941–1943*, Persephone Books, 1999. Reproduced by permission of the Random House Group Ltd.

WCC Publications for the prayer by an African Christian taken from *With All God's People: The New Ecumenical Prayer Cycle*, World Council of Churches, 1989

The Rt Revd Kenneth Cragg

The Corrymeela Community, Northern Ireland

Acknowledgements

Crossroad Publications

Wild Goose Publications, The Iona Community

SCM-Canterbury Press for permission to use a short extract from 'Morning Prayers' in Dietrich Bonhoeffer, *Letters and Papers from Prison*, SCM Press, 1971, p. 140

Mrs Sarah D. Jeffrey-Gray for permission to use the prayer by R. E. C. Browne

SPCK for permission to use material by Janet Morley, Eric Milner-White, George Appleton, The St Hilda Community, Kathy Galloway, Ralston Smith and Bishop Peter Lee

Introduction

This book really began as a series of newspaper columns. The *Church Times* once asked me to contribute a number of weekly columns entitled 'Prayer for the Week', in which I would reproduce a prayer and then write a short commentary upon it which would explain it and encourage people to use it. This column continues, now written by a large number of different people. This book contains 52 such reflections, one for each week of the year, including several of the original columns from the *Church Times*.

At that point the then Dean of Wells retired and I was asked to be the Acting Dean. We thought this would last for three or four months at most while a new Dean was chosen, but in fact it went on for eighteen months. So, while this was an interesting and creative time in the cathedral, it did mean that little could be done to complete the commissioned book and it has been inordinately delayed.

The book will now come to light after I have retired but inevitably it includes a number of references to Wells Cathedral, its worship and its beautiful building, which only shows just how much of an impression that building makes on anybody who works or worships there. I am profoundly glad and grateful to have been there.

I am also grateful to my editor at SPCK, Alison Barr, for her patience – and indeed for persuading me at one point not to drop the whole enterprise. I am also grateful to my wife June, who believed that I could do it even though our eyes were, by that time, firmly fixed on the heavenly city of my retirement.

I have been accompanied on this journey by a number of friends who were interested in the project and who suggested prayers, often their favourites, or ones that had become important to them, for inclusion in the book. In particular, I would like to thank Jean Moore, Paul Kelly, Hugh Dickinson, Peter Thorburn and Vanda Venn, whose suggestions have been included here together with a number of others whom I have had to disappoint.

I should say that the purpose of the book is to encourage people to pray reflectively. Readers should find a prayer they like and read it, pray it, think about it and savour it before God. The hope is that this will enrich their prayer life and make it less mechanical, more thoughtful and, hopefully, more contemplative. The choice of prayers is entirely mine. Many I have come to love through using them at Morning or Evening Prayer in Wells Cathedral. Others I have chosen because they reflected what I wanted to say or had come to think about a particular issue. In the end I found that much of what I wanted to say welled up from within my own being, and so I wrote a number of the prayers myself. In many ways I would have liked the book to be far more of a multi-media experience than is possible. I would have liked pictures or photographs and musical extracts to accompany each prayer as the page is turned and the prayer read so that the whole experience of praying is not simply verbal and goes, as George Herbert said, 'beyond the din of words'. I will have to leave readers to use their imaginations to supplement my gropings.

As I searched through the many books of prayers on my shelves I became conscious of a long stream of praying that I had done over many years and was thankful for it because I realized afresh how much I had been sustained on my journey. I also became conscious that there was a predominant theme in what I felt prayer was about. Prayer seems to me to be an expression of, and a crying out for, a new and different life which only comes from God but which, once known or tasted, transfigures everything else.

I gladly dedicate this book to my youngest grandchild, Ben Tomek, with the prayer that God's life may be his also.

Melvyn Matthews

TWO MORNING PRAYERS

O God, who hast folded back the mantle of the night to clothe us in the golden glory of the day, chase from our hearts all gloomy thoughts, and make us glad with the brightness of hope, that we may effectively aspire to unwon virtues, through Jesus Christ our Lord.

Morning Prayer, Gregorian Sacramentary, sixth century

I used this beautiful morning prayer at Matins in Wells Cathedral. There, at that time, the light streams into the quire through the fourteenth-century Golden Window above our heads. Christ and his Mother, portrayed in the window, bless us with their presence. There the child Jesus holds in his hand the apple which was the cause of our fall, saying, as it were, I have it safe now, all things are well. The light falls on the honey-coloured stone and everything is lit with the glory of the morning. It never fails to lift my spirits and, I am sure, the spirits of those who worship there. This quire is full of light at whatever time you enter it – you never feel trapped or enclosed when you are there – but it is also intimate enough to enable worshippers to feel held in the hand of God as they sit and pray in the medieval stalls as people have done for the last nine hundred years.

So much of the Christian faith is about light; the light of the morning streaming in symbolizes the light of Christ streaming in to dispel fear and sin and guilt. The Christian faith is about the joy of newness and hope, of knowing and believing that life is entirely a gift from God and being thankful that this is the case. My mother used to say that depression was a sin; I don't think that was true, for she spoke before a full understanding of mental illness became widespread, but her point was to do with gloominess and our attitude to life. Joy is possible whatever our circumstances, for it is a recognition that life is a gift.

My own response to this prayer is to resolve to allow that joy to permeate my encounters with other people. They too are a gift to me, whoever they are and whatever they may bring, however, at times, unwelcome. So as people come to me or as I approach them I try to see them new, to see them as if lit with the light of God and so bringing some new light to me. This is difficult and not always successful. My moods colour the encounter as much as their condition, but the faith we have is that these moods are not the final truth about ourselves. The final truth is that Christ's light inhabits us and our world. The question and the challenge is whether we choose that light and life or not.

In the Hebrew Scriptures the book of Deuteronomy purports to be Moses' speech to the children of Israel as they enter the Promised Land. Moses himself will not enter, so he gives them his last words. At the end of the speech he says,

> See, I have set before you today life and prosperity, death and adversity . . . I have set before you life and death, blessings and curses. Choose life so that you and your descendants may live. (Deuteronomy 30.15)

I believe the same choice is before faithful people today. We live in difficult, if not terrible, times. We are tempted to convey death and destruction upon others and upon ourselves, either by war or by selfishness. We will only do this while we refuse to accept that life is gift from elsewhere, from God.

Lord Jesu Christ, very sun of the world, ever arising and never going down; who by thine appearing giveth health and gladness, creating, preserving and nourishing all things in heaven and in earth; I pray thee graciously to enlighten my spirit, that the night of sin and the mists of error may be driven away by thine inward shining; so that I may go all my life long without stumbling, and walk in the daytime, pure and undefiled by the works of darkness; who with the Father and the Holy Spirit livest and reignest for ever.

Erasmus, 1467–1536

This prayer exists in a shorter and simpler form in the Elizabethan Primer of 1559, but I prefer this original version because the language is richer. It also contains a richer theology of the creation in which Christ is truly the sun which enlightens all things and not just the soul of man. Indeed in this prayer the illumination of the spirit which is prayed for is derived from, and secondary to, the illumination of all things. The version in the 1559 Primer omits the references to Christ as the light of all things. And I love 'thine inward shining' rather than the simpler 'inward light' of the later version. 'Inward shining' is much more powerful.

First of all this is a humble man's prayer. It reveals a humility of spirit which accepts that there are things which it does not know but needs to know. There is no trace of arrogance in it – but rather a recognition of lack and the possibility of falling. It is also a scholar's prayer, which knows the value of intellectual illumination. And a scholar, of course, is what Erasmus was. He was one of the greatest scholars of his day and read the Fathers of the Church in their original Greek and translated the Greek New Testament. But although he was deeply critical of the medieval Church and by his linguistic studies facilitated the Reformation, he was never a reformer. He constantly sought truth and an illumined mind and heart as this prayer reveals.

It is the spirit of Erasmus that this prayer recalls – a spirit of both scholarship and devotion. These two are necessary to each other. For most of the history of the Church, to be a theologian was to be a devout and prayerful person, but that is no longer understood to be necessary. The devout life and the scholarly life have been separated.

This is much to the impoverishment of both. Erasmus' life was a witness to the integration of prayer and scholarship.

But what I love most about the prayer is the petition that 'I may go all my life long without stumbling, and walk as in the daytime'. The assumption here is that darkness is a form of illusion, some form of shadow side. Indeed the phrase 'mists of error' confirms this. There is – as there was in Erasmus' day – a common assumption that misunderstanding is somehow natural to man, that sin is a natural state. Erasmus' prayer speaks of illumination as being our natural birthright. But we stumble, he says, perhaps because we do not look up and allow our path to be illumined, or accept that it is illumined already by Christ, the bright morning star, and our task is to open our eyes.

In spite of its age this is really a prayer which modern men and women need to know and pray regularly as an antidote to modern hubris and pessimism.

PRAYERS FOR ADVENT, CHRISTMAS, NEW YEAR AND EPIPHANY

Let me love thee, O Christ,
in thy first coming,
when thou wast made man, for love of men,
and for love of me.

Let me love thee, O Christ,
in thy second coming, when with an inconceivable love
thou standest and knockest at the door,
and wouldest enter into the souls of men,
and into mine.

Plant in my soul, O Christ, thy likeness of love;
that when by death thou callest,
it may be ready,
and burning
to come unto thee.

Advent Prayer, Eric Milner-White,
from *My God, My Glory*

The genius of this Advent prayer is that it brings together all of the 'comings' of Christ, in the past, in the present and in the future. There is no sense that Christ will only really come in the future. It recognizes that he comes now. Time is eternal in the work of God, what he does once he does always. It also makes no distinction between men and women in general and the person praying. What happens to all, happens to one, and what happened then is always happening.

The interesting metaphor is the metaphor of standing and knocking. It comes of course from the Revelation of St John the Divine where Jesus says, 'Behold, I stand at the door and knock' (Revelation 3.20) and is a traditional metaphor in Advent prayers, speaking of the coming of Christ and his wish to enter into our lives. It is a very courteous image. The Lord does not enter without first asking and then being invited to come in. He respects who we are and our capacity to refuse him entry. The medieval mystery plays portrayed Christ as going down to Hades to release the souls trapped there, but knocking first to announce his coming.

The most beautiful use of this image is made by the English poet Henry Vaughan in his striking poem 'The Night'. Here he reflects on the coming of Nicodemus to Jesus 'by night' (John 3.2). He speaks of the night as the time of opportunity, and writes,

> Dear night! This world's defeat;
> The stop to busy fools, care's check and curb;
> . . .
> God's silent, searching flight:
> When my Lord's head is filled with dew, and all
> His locks are wet with the clear drops of night;
> His still, soft call;
> His knocking time; the soul's dumb watch,
> When spirits their fair kindred catch.

'God's silent, searching flight' compares God to a night owl, flying silently over the countryside looking for the one he loves and calling, softly, as if with a still, small voice. The lines then move into imagery taken directly from the Song of Songs (5.10ff.), but then the night is spoken of as 'God's knocking time', the time when, in the dark, the Lord comes to speak and ask for love.

It is not easy for us to understand God as needing us; Christian devotion has concentrated more on our need for God, but several devotional writers speak of God as needy, as creating out of need, as coming to us out of need, simply because that is his nature. He knocks because he needs our love. Advent is the time of God's need as well as our own.

We thought we knew where to find you;
 we hardly needed a star to guide the way,
just perseverance and common sense;
why do you hide yourself away from the powerful
and join the refugees and outcasts,
calling us to follow you there?

> Wise God, give us wisdom.

We thought we had laid you safe in the manger;
we wrapped you in the thickest sentiment we could find,
and stressed how long ago you came to us;
why do you break upon us in our daily life
with messages of peace and goodwill,
demanding that we do something about it?

> Just and righteous God, give us justice and righteousness.

So where else would we expect to find you
but in the ordinary place with the faithful people,
turning the world to your purpose through them.
Bring us to that manger, to that true rejoicing,
which will make wisdom, justice and righteousness alive
 in us.

Stephen Orchard

———◆———

This excellent Christmas prayer unwraps all of the selfishness, sentiment and false high-mindedness with which we surround that feast.
It reminds us that our own belief in our own capacity to come to the
truth is actually an exercise of power and that Christ did not lodge
with the powerful. It reminds us that sentiment is no substitute for
real expressions of goodwill and the proper exercise of justice and
righteousness. It reminds us of the need to look more carefully at the
ordinary things of life, things which are hidden from us by a strange
but lethal combination of selfishness and sentiment.

The problem with celebrating Christmas in a rich western country is not so much the amount we spend or the waste which occurs

at this time, although all those things are deeply irreligious, but our inability to be with the ordinary and to be thankful for that – ordinary people, ordinary things, ordinary events. It is this stress on the ordinary that I find so welcome in this prayer. We do not value the simple and the ordinary as we should, and have to be led back to them. The reason we should value the ordinary is simply because it was in a very ordinary place that Christ was born, among very ordinary people and in the midst of the everyday occasion of a census.

There is a tendency in humanity to constantly require the extraordinary, the new, the experiential. This affects the Church as well as society. Religious people are just as sensation-seeking as everybody else – indeed perhaps more so because they believe that others will be more easily convinced of the truth of their claims if they make an extraordinary impact. Media evangelists are guilty of this tendency but so also are those trying to impress young people with the nature of religious faith. Such a quest drains our energies and limits our capacity for loving the ordinary and so for giving justice to the poor. When we crave the extraordinary we are the victims of our own capacity for self-illusion. Once we can see through that we shall more easily be able to serve those whom God wishes us to serve – namely the poor and the ordinary people of this world.

M y Father, I abandon myself to you. Do with me as you will. Whatever you may do with me I thank you. I am prepared for anything. I accept everything, provided your will is fulfilled in me and in all creatures. I ask for nothing more, my God. I place my soul in your hands. I give it to you, my God, with all the love of my heart, because I love you. And for me it is a necessity of love, this gift of myself, this placing of myself in your hands without reserve in boundless confidence, because you are my Father.

Charles de Foucauld, 1858–1916

I used to hear words similar to these each New Year when I was a boy. I was brought up as a Methodist and each New Year would attend with my mother the Methodist Covenant Service. During that service the people pledge themselves to a faithful life for the coming year and say,

> I am no longer my own, but Thine. Put me to what thou wilt, rank me with whom thou wilt . . . I freely and heartily yield all things to thy pleasure and disposal. And now, O glorious and blessed God, Father, Son and Holy Spirit, thou art mine and I am Thine . . .

So although Charles de Foucauld's prayer might sound extreme, and one perhaps only for those taking religious vows, it is also part of a more widespread Christian tradition in which faithful people give themselves over to the will of God in their lives and seek by this act of commitment to free themselves from their own selfishness.

This was certainly part of Charles de Foucauld's own desire. He was a French aristocrat who, after an abortive career in the army, experienced a traumatic conversion and gave himself to life with the poorest of the poor. He lived for a time in the Holy Land but eventually dedicated himself to the people of the Sahara Desert and lived among the Tuareg, translating the scriptures into their language and serving their needs. He followed a very ascetic rule of life and tried to attract others into a community life with him, but without success.

Since his death, however, the communities of the Little Brothers and Sisters of Jesus have become an established part of the Christian witness. They are people who have decided, in a phrase they use, to 'cry the gospel with their life' and live among the poorest people of the world in a simple act of witness. Their lives effectively symbolize the presence of Christ among his children.

So as I say this prayer I remember several groups of people. I remember the Methodist people, among whom I grew up and who gave me the faith, and ask that they be kept faithful to their way of witness after the example of John Wesley. I remember with thanksgiving Charles de Foucauld himself and his present-day followers working and living with the poorest of God's children 'in order to keep the rumour of God alive' among them. I ask for grace for myself that I may give my life afresh to God each day in thankfulness, living a life of simplicity and trust.

A lmighty God, who hast planted the daystar in the heavens, and scattering the night, dost restore morning to the world, fill us, we beseech thee, with thy mercy, so that thou being our enlightener, all the darkness of our sins may be dispersed, through our Lord, Jesus Christ.

Collect for Epiphany, Sarum Breviary

This is a collect for Epiphany from one of the old English rites, the Sarum Breviary. The Epiphany is the most beautiful of the Church's feasts, sadly reduced these days to little more than a celebration of the arrival of the Magi at the stable. In the earlier days of the Church, and still in the East, Epiphany celebrates the baptism of Christ by John the Baptist and also the first of his miracles as recorded by St John, the turning of the water into wine at Cana in Galilee, both incidents which manifest or reveal his hidden glory. The importance of the celebration of the Magi is that they followed the star, and this incident derives its luminosity and strength from the words in Isaiah, 'Arise, shine, for your light has come, and the glory of the Lord has risen upon you . . . Nations shall come to your light, and kings to the brightness of your dawn' (Isaiah 60.1, 3).

So this ancient prayer celebrates the Epiphany of Christ by using the most beautiful imagery of Christ the daystar or morning star who scatters the darkness to restore morning to the world. The pre-Reformation Church always saw Christ as exercising a cosmic role in the life of the universe. He was not simply a figure of history to whom we had to relate by reflection or prayer, but somebody who was actually at the heart of all things, the principle of life, the inner life of things, the word or wisdom which God speaks in all things who, when he rises as the daystar on high, dispels the darkness of the world.

We should not be afraid, in this scientific age, to use such imagery. It is not in conflict with a scientific understanding and indeed enhances the role of science by showing that the scientific and religious quests are both quests for meaning in what is to hand. Is the universe coherent? Is there a principle or force at work which holds it all together? The cosmic understanding of Christ affirms that there is such inner meaning to things, hidden and secret, but present and real.

One contemporary scientist who struggled to recapture some-thing of the godwardness of things is Annie Dillard, the young American biologist, who spent a year in the Appalachian Moun-tains struggling with the complexities of nature and its apparent cruelty and dissonance. But at the end of her account (*Pilgrim at Tinker Creek*) she knows that the universe is not chaotic but rather a strange outpouring, a stream of life for which the only response is thankfulness.

> I think that the dying pray at the last, not 'please', but 'thank you', as a guest thanks his host at the door . . . Divinity is not playful. The universe is not made in jest but in solemn incomprehensible earnest. By a power that is unfathomably secret and holy and fleet. There is nothing to be done about it, but ignore it, or see. And then you walk fearlessly . . .

A recognition that the universe has at its heart Christ the morning star enables us to live fearlessly and with and for those who have much without desiring as much or to live with and for those who have nothing without falling into the mistake of thinking that their salvation lies in having all things. All of us have all things already.

Mary, Mother of Jesus,
walk through life with us
whom he called his sisters and his brothers.

And, as a sword pierced your own heart,
be a healing presence to all
whose lives are pierced with grief and loss.

In the power of Jesus your Son,
our Risen Lord.

Hugh Dickinson

Hugh Dickinson, the author of this prayer, was Dean of Salisbury Cathedral and was inspired to write this prayer by the bronze statue of Mary on the green in front of the cathedral. This statue is called *The Walking Madonna* and is by Elizabeth Frink, one of the foremost of English sculptors, and it is an exceptionally strong and striking portrayal, especially as Mary is placed striding away from the cathedral just as you, the visitor, are walking towards it. 'Why is she going away?' you think, and, 'Why is she striding away so purposefully?' The statue also portrays Mary as an older woman, not elderly, but older than many portrayals of her and to some extent careworn, certainly somebody who has experienced grief. When I see this statue, which I do regularly, I always think she is striding away from the cross.

I think our surprise at this statue is because we have been brought up to see Mary as mild and obedient. She is the one who bows her head to the angel and says 'Yes', submissively. And sadly, this has been understood by many to be the model for women's behaviour in the Church. Yet there is another strand of reflection about Mary, which it may be Elizabeth Frink has picked up, which sees her as a strong woman responding to the enormous demands that bearing this child and bringing him up puts upon her. She is the one who says 'Yes' boldly, who grasps an enormous task with both hands and who knows from the beginning that none of it will be easy. One way of understanding Jesus the strong teacher, the one defiant before Pilate in Jerusalem, is to say, 'This man must have had a remarkable mother.'

Mary was a strong woman who bore pain and grief, who struggled to come to terms with whatever it was that was demanded of her by God, but who, in the end, embraced it. She strides away from the cross in order to strengthen others, to ask us to come to the cross and gain courage to bear, and to defy and to live with the pain that life brings in order to bring goodness out of it. She strides away from the cathedral in order to tell us that piety can be a trap and that what is needed is strong discipleship in God's world.

She is full of grace and truth, but she knows that this is earned at no little cost and asks us to brace ourselves to bear the same in our own day.

PRAYERS FOR LENT AND
PASSIONTIDE

L ord, remember not only the men and women of good will, but also those of ill will. But, do not remember all of the suffering they have inflicted upon us: instead remember the fruits we have borne because of this suffering – our fellowship, our loyalty to one another, our humility, our courage, our generosity, the greatness of heart that has grown from this trouble. When our persecutors come to be judged by you, let all of these fruits that we have borne be their forgiveness.

> Source unknown (found in the clothing of a dead child at
> Ravensbruck concentration camp)

This prayer is about the uses of adversity, the good that God brings out of evil. We usually find it difficult to see how anything good can come out of evil, especially when it inflicts itself upon us. Certainly we find it difficult to see how anything good could have come out of the Holocaust. This prayer should give us pause and it is worth trying to make it our own when we are in the midst of suffering.

I remember once interviewing the great Rabbi Hugo Gryn, who had escaped death at Auschwitz as a child but whose father had perished. We were talking about the Joseph story in the Old Testament where Joseph is sold into slavery by his brothers. For Hugo Gryn, as for many Jews, this is a story about the Holocaust and Egypt symbolizes the concentration camps which the Jewish people had to endure. During the interview Hugo Gryn said,

> Joseph is the example for us of how you can grow in and through adversity. Mind you, I don't think that is the only way to grow. My preferred way of growing is to be born into a nice family with a loving mother and father . . . Well, that's nice, but that was not the case that happened with Joseph, and indeed in Jewish history, the Joseph kind of development was the one we encounter more frequently.

In the Joseph story terrible things happen. A group of brothers conspire to murder their younger brother. They just manage to hold back from this, but allow him to be sold to passing merchants and then lie to their father to cover up their complicity. It's the sort of story you see in an American gangster film. But then at the end of the story the brothers are forced by famine to seek food in Egypt

23

and come face to face with their brother who is the lord of the grain stores. In the end Joseph reveals himself to his brothers and says, 'Do not be afraid, God was at work in all of this. God sent me before you to preserve life.' By now Joseph has had time to reflect upon what had happened between him and his brothers and how that whole terrible tragedy, the loss and the lying, was redeemed by a hidden inner purpose. Something else was going on as well which was more powerful but which they could not see at the time.

This was what the unknown writer of that prayer somehow understood. This is not the way we would prefer to develop; we would prefer to grow quietly, nicely, comfortably. The trouble is that comfortable circumstances do not always produce goodness and courage, comfort can and does prevent that happening. Similarly hardship is not always something which generates goodness and love. Sometimes it destroys.

But if we are patient in suffering and accept it and work with it, then God's overwhelming purposes can work through it and we will become stronger where we are broken.

I've been inspired recently by a woman I visited for three years who had incurable cancer. She has now died. During her illness, which she called her affliction, she would say to me, 'My affliction causes love to flourish. It draws love out of me for my family and friends, for I know I do not have much more time with them, and it draws love out of them, for they come to visit me and bring me gifts and show me love.'

Perhaps she knew about this prayer.

O Christ, as we walk through the land that you loved, in the country where you lived and taught, grant us the grace and wisdom to see clearly and understand deeply that all you suffered was for the sake of redeeming humanity. Through your life, death and resurrection, you have made it possible for us to have life, and have it more abundantly.

> O Christ, as we follow you down the road to Calvary,
> Guide us to become active participants, not curious
>   bystanders.
> O Christ, as we stand with the mourners at the Cross,
> Give us the love that can forgive those who trespass against
>   us.
> O Christ, as we witness the new life given to us through
>   your resurrection,
> Empower us with faith to act and spread the Good News.
>
> Palestinian women of Jerusalem

I think this is a moving and wonderfully courageous prayer, written as it is by women who have suffered so much at the hands of others. Homes have been bulldozed, husbands, fathers and brothers killed, imprisoned without trial, interrogated. Employment restricted, movement curtailed . . . and still they can pray, asking to become active participants in the suffering of Christ, and can say that they are witnesses to the new life given them through the resurrection. One is tempted to ask what new life?

My wife and I first went to the Holy Land in the 1960s when I was still a theological student. We flew into Jerusalem and took a bus to Nazareth, where we were sure that a Christian hostel would have a bed for the night. Unfortunately they had been visited by an enormous group of French Catholics and were all completely full. A Palestinian young man said that he would take us on to the next hostel, which, he was sure, would have places. It did not. On the spur of the moment and without any consultation – after all this was before the arrival of mobile phones – he invited us to stay in his family house. His family were Syrian Uniate Catholics who retained the Orthodox liturgy but were loyal to Rome. So we slept on the floor, with a photograph of the Pope on one wall and the Syrian Patriarch on the other!

We were made so welcome and were asked to return for a few days at the end of our tour of the Holy Land. We learned at first hand of the restrictions on Palestinians even that long ago. The situation is far, far worse now and many Palestinian Christians, who see themselves as being a Christian presence in the Holy Land since the time of Christ, have moved abroad, so that the community is now very small.

What such a community does – which is illustrated by this prayer – is to be the body of Christ. So they bear the pain and receive the risen life. They are true witnesses to the life of Christ simply by being who they are and suffering what they do. The most moving petition in this prayer is that, as they follow Christ down the road to Calvary (which some of them do, literally, every day), they should be active participants, not curious bystanders. I think this is a prayer which so many of us need to make and to accept as part of the vocation of the Christian in today's world. The redemption of the world did not simply happen once and for all a long time ago, as if we could now sit back and just be thankful for what we have received. Christians are active participants in the redeeming work of Christ. They do not just receive it or believe 'Jesus saves', they actually bear the pain themselves and by that participation actively share in the work of redeeming the world. They, like us, are Christ's body and called to share in what he does, now.

Jesus, each of us is both the thief who blasphemes
And the one who believes.
I have faith, Lord, help my lack of faith.
I am nailed to death, there is nothing I can do,
but cry out: 'Jesus, remember me
when you come with your kingdom.'

Jesus, I know nothing, I understand nothing
in this horrific world.
But you, you come to me, with open arms,
with open heart,
and your presence alone is my paradise.
Ah, remember me
when you come with your kingdom.

Glory and praise to you, you who welcome
not the healthy but the sick,
you whose unexpected friend is a criminal
cut off by the justice of men.
Already you are going down to hell and setting free
those who cry out to you:
'Remember us, Lord,
when you come with your kingdom.'

Ecumenical Patriarch Bartholomew of the Orthodox Church

I love this prayer for a number of reasons. It takes the horror of living in today's world seriously. It sees it as the cross we have to bear today. It also focuses on what to my mind is the central purpose of the cross, namely the embrace of that suffering world by God in Christ. He stretches out his arms upon the cross in order to embrace, hold to himself and thereby draw the sting of the suffering of the world. That is how it is done. And so the phrases, 'I am nailed to death', 'this horrific world', express the reality of experience for all of us now. But then after an acknowledgement of that reality comes the mercy of the open arms, the open heart, the welcome for the sick, the friendship with the criminal, all of which crystallizes the central meaning of what is going on in this crucifixion of Jesus.

The cross is where God embraces a suffering world, revealing that his love is greater than the suffering and evil we endure, and so begins the process of redemption. Our response to that embrace is to share in the work of redemption by ourselves turning to embrace the suffering we witness.

Then at the end of this prayer Patriarch Bartholomew refers to the Harrowing of Hell by Jesus. This is a frequent Orthodox theme but one which is not so common in the Western church. In Orthodoxy it is this which constitutes the resurrection (called *anastasis*, 'the standing up') rather than simply the resurrection of Christ on his own. Wall paintings and mosaics portray this event by depicting Christ trampling on the gates of hell, driving out the devils and reaching for the hand of Adam and Eve, the prototype human beings, and leading them out from the underworld followed by those who have been captive. There is a remarkable twelfth-century mosaic of the Harrowing of Hell on the west wall of the cathedral of Torcello, situated on one of the islands in the Venetian Lagoon. Here Christ grasps Adam by the wrist and is accompanied by John the Baptist, these two men being the first and last persons of the time before the arrival of Christ, the Liberator. Interestingly the contemporary children's writer Philip Pullman depicts a similar release of souls from hell in his novel *The Amber Spyglass*, and so the theme has not died.

In many ways this is a much more inclusive understanding of the victory of Christ, and it is reflected in this prayer, which repeats the cry of those who long for release from death, 'Remember us Lord, when you come with your kingdom.'

For the darkness of waiting
of not knowing what is to come
of staying ready and quiet and attentive,
we praise you O God.

For the darkness and the light
are both alike to you.

For the darkness of staying silent
for the terror of having nothing to say
and for the greater terror
of needing to say nothing,
we praise you O God.

For the darkness and the light
are both alike to you.

For the darkness of loving
in which it is safe to surrender
to let go of our self-protection
and to stop holding back our desire,
we praise you O God.

For the darkness and the light
are both alike to you.

For the darkness of choosing
when you give us the moment
to speak, and act, and change,
and we cannot know what we have set in motion,
but we still have to take the risk,
we praise you O God.

For the darkness and the light
are both alike to you.

For the darkness of hoping
in a world which longs for you,

for the wrestling and the labouring of all creation
for wholeness and justice and freedom,
we praise you O God.

For the darkness and the light
are both alike to you.

Janet Morley

This is really one of my favourite prayers and, in my view, one of the best prayers to have been written in today's Church. It says so much about the importance of waiting and silence, of the unknown but continuing work of God when we have done all we can, that everybody should know it. It should be placed on the desk of anybody who ministers in the Church today, whether as preacher or as pastor, for today's Church is so full of the importance of knowing and speaking the truth that saying this prayer regularly will remind us of the way in which 'unknowing' is not a negative but rather a positive force in our lives.

Let us linger with this for a moment. John Keats, in a famous letter, wrote about 'negative capability', saying,

> Negative Capability, that is when a man is capable of being in uncertainties, mysteries, doubts, without any irritable reaching after fact and reason.

Another poet, Rilke, said a similar thing in another letter, this time to a young poet who had written to him. Rilke says,

> I do entreat you as strongly as I can, my dear Sir, to stay patient with all that is unresolved in your own heart, to try to love the very questions, just as if they were locked up rooms or as if they were books in an utterly unknown language. You ought not yet to be searching for answers, for you could not yet live them.

Both these poets knew something of the importance of waiting in darkness for answers to be given rather than striven for. Both also knew that when that happened much truer answers were eventually found, even though they were quite different and quite unexpected. To come to that point is real spiritual wisdom.

But another reason I love this prayer is for its recognition of those moments of unknowing to which we are all heir and which are apparently terrifying. Not least among these are the moments of not having anything to say, what the prayer calls, 'The darkness of staying silent for the terror of having nothing to say and for the greater terror of needing to say nothing'. The greatness of these lines is to be found in the reassurance they give that silence also speaks. It is not a negative force to be controlled or regulated by human beings who believe that only words or activity are real. It is to be allowed because our words and our activity are partial and often unseeing. We need silence in order for greater realities than those we know to become part of what is happening to us. Modern people find this difficult. I'm afraid I have got to the point where I judge a person by his capacity to remain comfortably silent in company, for such a person has an interior surety which is not weakness, not uncertainty, but simple confidence either that it is not necessary to speak or that more speaking will only further cheapen what has been said. Such a person has learned that silence is also a way of speaking.

The two thanksgivings, for 'the darkness of loving' and 'the darkness of choosing', are also important. They ask us to remember that those moments when we let go into love or make a choice, even though we do not know what the outcomes will be, are part of human maturity. To be people who refuse to allow such moments in our lives is constantly to live as infants, believing that the rationality of light is better than the darkness of unknowing. The Christian spiritual tradition has never accepted that that is the case.

I quoted Rilke just now. He says, in another letter to that young poet,

> We have no grounds for suspicion of our world, for it is not hostile to us. If there are terrors then they are our terrors, if chasms, then those chasms too are ours; if there are dangers then it is for us to learn to love them . . . Perhaps everything of terror in our lives is in its deepest nature a helpless thing that craves our help.

This prayer reminds us of that.

O Loving Saviour, we would linger by thy cross, that the light of thy perfect love may shine into the secret places of our souls, showing what is vile there, so that it may shrink away, and nurturing whatever there is pure or lovely or of good report, so that beholding thee, we may become more like thee, thou revealer of God to men, thou guide of men to God.

William Temple

I used this prayer and the next one whenever I conducted the Stations of the Cross during Lent or Holy Week. In Wells Cathedral there is a lovely set of fourteen icons of the Stations of the Cross painted by a contemporary iconographer, Sylvia Dimitrova. These are hung in the nave during Lent, and each Friday people follow the way of the cross in heart and mind, and go, as if accompanying Christ on the first Good Friday, from station to station remembering the traditional incidents and praying through this last journey. My custom was to use this prayer at the end of the little devotional act at each icon.

I used it because it strikes just the right note about the cross of Christ. For me the cross is not a doctrine to be unravelled, with the question posed, 'Why did Christ die on the cross?' with then a long exposition as to how that happened – rather it is a point of revelation, an opening of a window into the true nature of God. Through this window the light of truth shines, and if we can we must linger there so that this fierce light can show us the truth about ourselves and reveal to us the truth about God. So I do not want to think about the cross as if it were a theological puzzle to be unravelled but I want to linger at the cross, to be there and allow its brilliant but astringent light into my life.

Thomas Traherne, who was a country parson in Herefordshire at the time of the Restoration, thought of the cross in this way. He said,

> The cross of Christ is the Jacob's ladder by which we ascend into the highest heavens. That cross is a tree set on fire with invisible flame, that illuminateth the whole world. The flame is love . . . in the light of which we see how to possess all the things in heaven and earth after his similitude.

In his meditation on the cross Traherne quotes Jesus' words from St John's Gospel, 'I, if I be lifted up, will draw all people unto me', and makes the cross the central point of divine attraction, where God's 'wanting' of us, and our 'wanting' of God, which God's 'wanting' has, mysteriously, placed in our hearts, come together. In this way God draws us with the cords of love and draws us deeper into his light and love.

This process is a difficult one, for it means allowing that love of God to purge us of all that is unloving in us and allowing ourselves to be released from our pleasures in order to return to God, our home. That is what is happening in the Christian's faith in the cross. It is a process not a belief.

O Lord Jesus Christ, whose unjust judgement we justly con-
demn, save us from all malice and uncharitableness in
accusing our brethren, lest what we do unto others we do unto you,
and doom you afresh, our Saviour and God for ever and ever.

Eric Milner-White, from *A Procession of Passion Prayers*

———◆——

When I was a teenager I was fond of the cinema – indeed I have
remained very fond of it ever since – and was deeply impressed by
the film *On the Waterfront*, which I must have seen when I was
about fifteen years old. It remains a classic film. The Director was
Elia Kazan, with a young Marlon Brando as a longshoreman who
tries to stand up to the corruption of the union bosses. There is
a memorable scene where somebody is killed and lies spreadeagled
on the deck of a ship with his arms outstretched as if he has been
crucified, and Brando stands there and berates those responsible. He
says something to the effect that every time they kill somebody then
Jesus Christ is crucified over again. I remember this because it helped
me, as a young teenager with a religious upbringing, to understand
the meaning of the crucifixion; but it also illustrates perfectly the
understanding of the cross behind this prayer.

There are two things to say. First, and most important, that whatever we do to each other we also do to Christ, who lives in each one
of us. So the crucifixion of one man is also the crucifixion of Christ.
Looking at things this way takes the incarnation utterly seriously.
Others have had the same understanding, especially Mother Teresa
and her Sisters of Charity. The Sisters care for the dying in the slums
of Calcutta, and they are taught to see each person who is brought in
as Christ himself, and to touch and speak to them as if they were
touching and speaking to Christ. Of course, there is precedent for
this in the Gospels. In the parable of the sheep and the goats Jesus
says,

> I was hungry and you gave me food, I was thirsty and you gave me
> something to drink, I was a stranger and you welcomed me . . . Truly I
> tell you, just as you did it to one of the least of these who are members
> of my family, you did it to me. (Matthew 25.35)

St Benedict, in his instructions to his monks in the Rule of Benedict, urges them to receive guests at the monastery as if they were Christ himself. So the kindnesses or the injustices which we mete out to others we actually mete out to Christ.

The other thing the prayer reminds us of is the need for justice in our dealings with each other. The word for justice or righteousness (in Hebrew *sadiq* and in Greek *dikaiosune*) permeates both the Hebrew Scriptures and the New Testament, always meaning that human beings are intended to live as God wants and in close relationship with him. To do this we must live in righteousness and justice with each other.

O Lord and Saviour, stripped naked upon your cross, yet robed eternally in holiness and light; take from us the rags of both our sins and our imagined righteousness; and clothe us with the mantle of your praises in Sion; where you are alive and reign in the glory of the Father and the Holy Spirit, ever one God, world without end.

Eric Milner-White, from *A Procession of Passion Prayers*

Here is another of the lovely Passion Prayers by Eric Milner-White, who was Dean of York during the Second World War. He wrote a large number of prayers, many of which have entered into the devotional life of the Church of England and are in regular use largely because of their simplicity and beauty, like this one. It is not so well known that Milner-White was a Chaplain to the Forces in the First World War and wrote of his experiences there in a book called *The Church in the Furnace*, in which he shared his conviction that the Church needed to speak more directly to the needs of the common man. The Book of Common Prayer, he concluded, was not enough. So he wrote his own prayers and caught the imagination of many people.

The imagery he uses here, of nakedness and clothing, is beautiful. I used this prayer when we came, in following the Stations of the Cross, to the point where Christ is stripped of his clothing. Christ's nakedness on the cross becomes a metaphor for our own need for spiritual nakedness and the need to lose our clothing of pride and to be clothed with praise alone.

Nor is this so far from the meaning of the stripping in the Gospels, particularly in Mark's Gospel. There are two particular incidents in Mark where people lose their clothes. In chapter 10, blind Bartimaeus asks Jesus for mercy, and Jesus calls him. 'So throwing off his cloak, he sprang up and came to Jesus.' Later on in the Garden of Gethsemane, there is the strange incident of the young man who had been following Jesus wearing nothing but a linen cloth. 'They caught hold of him, but he left the linen cloth and ran off naked.' For Mark 'stripping' has a spiritual meaning. It portrays something of the simplicity of self with which we must come before God. Bartimaeus and the young man leave behind them what they do not need, just as Jesus does when he goes to God by means of the cross.

Earlier in the Gospel Jesus sent the disciples out to preach and to heal. 'He ordered them to take nothing for their journey . . .'

I thought we ought to sing
A Lament, as we took his body down.
A song of weeping, rich and deep,
A pouring out of pain.

One like we used to sing in Chapel
On Sunday evenings long ago.
When the preacher couldn't get there,
And we'd sing, then, long and slow.

But the only song I could remember
Was a Negro song I knew,
One with deep black rhymes and rhythms,
From the bottom of my soul.

So I sang it as we lifted,
As we washed his arms and face,
I sang it with the women there,
From the bottom of our soul.

I sang it to my sweet Prince there,
From the bottom of my soul:

Go down Moses,
Go down to Egypt land . . .

Tell ol' Pharaoh,

Let my people go,

Let my people go . . .

Melvyn Matthews

I wrote this prayer poem when I was a parish priest. The Reader
in my parish was a talented woman who had been one of the GPs in
the village but was also an artist. She had made a sequence of draw-
ings for the Stations of the Cross, and during Holy Week these were

hung in the church. I wrote a sequence of poems to accompany them. This is the poem for the thirteenth station, 'Jesus is taken down from the Cross'.

I imagine that Jesus is taken down not just by Joseph of Arimathea but by the women who had stood by the cross and who had followed him in his ministry and who loved him. These words come from the mouth of Mary Magdalene, who in the Christian artistic tradition is shown standing next to Christ as he dies. She loves him, so she takes him down to prepare his body for burial. As she does so she wants to sing, and remembers a Negro spiritual. I see her as a nonconformist, Chapel rather than Church. In that tradition singing is important, and Chapel people, as I know, would sometimes have to wait for the preacher if he was delayed or prevented from coming, and would then sing their own songs.

But the spiritual that comes to her is one which speaks of redemption, the redemption of the people of Israel by Moses, who went down into Egypt to speak to 'Ol' Pharaoh'. This, of course, is a parable of Jesus' work on the cross. For in biblical imagery Egypt is the land of death and Moses is the Christlike figure who goes down into this land to redeem his people. So as Jesus descends from the cross he descends into Hades to call his people out of darkness into the light.

But the poem is not just about redemption, it is also about love, the love of Mary for Jesus. This is no more than hinted at in the Gospels. We are just beginning to see the importance of this sort of love in the Jesus story and in the history of Christian spirituality. We have been too long convinced that love is a practical matter, that it is a doing of love which matters. That is true, but should not be allowed to obscure the fact that every now and again the Gospels hint at the passionate love of people like Mary Magdalene. It should make us less timid about our loves, for all such passion comes from and returns to God.

PRAYERS FOR EASTER

Jesus, joy of our hearts, your Gospel assures us that the Kingdom of God is in our midst, and the gates of simplicity, and those of innocence, open within us.

Jesus our joy, the simple desire for your presence is already the beginning of faith. And, in our life, the hidden event of a longing causes wellsprings to gush forth: kindness, generosity, and also that inner harmony which comes from the Holy Spirit in us.

Bless us, Lord Christ; you give us a Gospel freshness when a heart that trusts is at the beginning of everything.

Saviour of every life, may those who seek you rejoice. You tell us: I am familiar with your trials and your poverty, and yet you are filled. Filled with what? With the living springs, hidden in your depths.

Jesus, love of all loving, in the ploughed-up earth of our lives you come to plant the trusting of faith. A small seed at first, faith can become within us one of the most unmistakable Gospel realities. It keeps alive the inexhaustible goodness of a human heart.

Bless us, Christ Jesus; your love comes to heal the wounds of our heart.

Brother Roger, Prior of the Taizé Community

———————

I first went to Taizé, in France, in the 1960s with a group of young people from Britain who were helping to build a youth centre in a city nearby. We poured concrete during the day and talked in the evenings. One day we were taken by our hosts to the fledgling monastic community in Taizé. French Protestants found this place amazing. Our hosts said, 'You Anglicans will love this. They kneel down to pray!' And in those days they did. Since then they have removed almost all of the furniture from the great church and use prayer stools. Most of the (largely young) congregation now sit on the floor to pray. During our visit one of the brothers spoke to us about the religious life, and we heard the remarkable story of the genesis of this community and the faithfulness of Brother Roger and his companions to the life of prayer and to a ministry of reconciliation. Over the years I returned to make a number of retreats there. One was in a small tent in the silent field adjoining the community church, where I spent the week reading a book about the Beatitudes, and I still remember it as a turning-point in my ministry.

This prayer by Brother Roger, the Prior of Taizé, speaks of what I first found in that community and which is still fresh for us now. As a result of those visits and retreats I became convinced that God was not so much far away, waiting for me to come to him, but very close by, within me somehow and perhaps 'nearer than breathing, closer than hands and feet . . .' I became aware that I was in danger of striving for salvation when salvation was being offered to me from within my own being by the Christ who was there waiting for me to discover him. I came to a sense of the presence of Christ deep within my existence – a presence that I had forgotten about, or perhaps found difficulty in believing was there, but which was actually sustaining me all the while and was hidden deep within all things.

But this prayer and those retreats also speak to me of how, because of our awareness of the presence of Christ in our lives, we then can turn and, with Christ in us, love others and be reconciled to them, because this is a possibility for us in our life with Christ. It is he who lives this life within us. Our task is to release that life from the depths of our being. The work of prayer and reconciliation, I have learned, is not so much mine to achieve as Christ's within me which I must allow full place in my life.

This prayer – and the life of the Taizé community behind it – reminds us that prayer which does not lead to an actual reconciled life is one where there is no 'sign of trust'. If we do not recognize that Christ is at work independent of our doubts or even of our faith, then what we are saying in effect is that our life is all our own and that we can see it all and know what it is all about. We admit by our lack of reconciliation not only that we do not trust but also that we think we know and can see everything that is at work in our lives. There is no mystery, no grace, nothing else than what we know about and can control. Somehow we cannot admit that Christ has occupied our hearts before we knew about him.

The good news about our lives is that Christ goes on working in us independently of what we know or do or even believe.

That is a real cause for joy. The question is, 'Can we believe it?'

O Christ, my Lord, again and again I have said with Mary Magdalene, 'They have taken away my Lord and I know not where they have laid him.'

I have been desolate and alone.

And you have found me again, and I know that what has died is not you, my Lord, but only my idea of you, the image which I have made to preserve what I have found, and to be my security.

I shall make another image, O Lord, better than the last. That, too, must go, and all successive images, until I come to the blessed vision of yourself, O Christ, my Lord.

George Appleton

A friend of mine suggested I include this prayer. She says, 'This has been of great comfort to me at difficult times.' I think it is a prayer of especial value to people, like my friend, who are sustained by the sensible comforts of religious faith – warm friendships, good music, rich liturgy, good conversation, imagery of all kinds. When these fail or are taken away or are overlaid by illness or physical disability, then it is almost as if Christ himself has been taken away and we cannot tell where they have laid him.

George Appleton's insight is to compare the desolate soul with Mary Magdalene, who was weeping outside of the tomb, lamenting the loss of her physical Lord. She could not, at least initially, see him in a new form, as her risen and transfigured Lord, and mistook him for the gardener. She had to learn that the loss of Christ in one form is only the re-appearance of Christ in another form.

There are parallels with this movement from, 'not this, but this and then again not even that, but this' in the Hindu tradition known as 'Advaita' – 'Not knowing'. And there are still more parallels in the Christian tradition known as 'the negative way', the way of un-knowing. In this prayer Archbishop Appleton describes the way of unknowing in simple, but telling terms.

Those who are puzzled by talk of the negative way have to re-member that God is not an object. He cannot be counted even as a spiritual being. He is rather beyond all knowing, beyond all description. This means that every attempt to talk about him has to be allowed to break down in the face of the truth about God. All imagery will fail, and unless we recognize that, we will be guilty of a form of idolatry. God cannot be directly described.

And so there is a gentle but nonetheless necessary process of purgation which has to go on in our awareness of God. We have to allow that because of his greatness he will always be beyond our reach but because of our finitude we are always constrained to speak about him in some way or another. This process of purgation is part of what it means to say 'I believe in God.'

Of course this process is difficult, sometimes painfully so, hence the weeping of Mary Magdalene with which my friend identified so closely. Jesus asked Mary not to cling to him, and Meister Eckhart, the German mystic, said the same. He encouraged his hearers, who were often women who sought spiritual experiences, to love God unspiritually. He said,

> You should love God. You should love God apart from his loveableness. You should love God unspiritually, that is your soul should be stripped of all spirituality, for as long as your soul has a spirit's form it has images and it has not unity or simplicity.

It is God we have to love, not our images of him. We have to be ready to let even the most precious images of God go if God is to be truly God in us.

G od of terror and joy,
you arise to shake the earth.
Open our graves
and give us back the past;
so that all that has been buried
may be freed and forgiven,
and our lives may return to you
through the risen Christ.

Janet Morley

This is a prayer to say at Eastertide. It derives its power from the fact that it plunges directly into our capacity to bury the past and to keep it sealed as comfort and identity. The prayer does not begin by referring to the resurrection of Jesus, it opens with a reference to God as the source of resurrection – which is exactly the point of the biblical accounts, for they say, 'God raised him . . .' – but it then makes the direct connection between that raising and the need for the graves of our past to be opened and freed.

Human beings have, it seems, an innate capacity to keep the past buried in their consciousness and to use that past against others. This is precisely what has been happening in Northern Ireland, where two versions of a buried past have conflicted. It is precisely what is happening in Israel/Palestine, where memories are equally long and buried but equally powerful. A recent radio programme, on which young Israelis were interviewed about the present conflict, said that every Israeli who had been asked to speak began by talking about history, Israeli history. For some this goes back to the biblical record. The Bible is used as a memory bank to prove the rightness of a particular cause.

The most urgent task facing communities caught in this sort of conflict is the healing of memory, the release of memory so that it can be forgiven and be a source of life rather than a source of conflict and disaster. In psychological terms this is what the resurrection of Jesus does now. W. H. Vanstone, the Anglican priest who so stirred the contemporary Church with his wonderful books *Love's Endeavour, Love's Expense* and *The Stature of Waiting*, was also a poet. In his last book, *Farewell in Christ*, he published a poem he had written some twenty years before the book in which it appeared was even thought of, in which he imagines Joseph of Arimathea burying Christ in the tomb of his memory so that he can keep the treasure of the past safe. The poem ends by Mary Magdalene announcing to him that Christ has risen from the tomb of memory so that he can be not only the past but also the future.

> He cannot rest content to be your past,
> So he has risen to be your future too.

Using Janet Morley's prayer at Easter will enable us to discern just how much we are acting out of our buried past, not allowing that past to be healed and forgiven and so living towards the future with new bright hopes instead of regret and resentment derived from buried history.

May Christ bring your past out of the tomb and so set you free to live with him now!

PRAYERS FOR PENTECOST

W̶e do not understand, eternal God,
the ways of your Spirit in the lives
of women and men.
She comes along secret paths
to take us unawares.
She touches us in joy and sorrow
to make us whole.
She hides behind coincidence
to lead us forward,
and uses human accidents
as occasions for influence.
We do not understand
but we welcome her presence
and rejoice in her power.

St Hilda Community

I like this prayer a lot and used it in public worship in the cathedral where I worked, partly I suspect because I liked surprising people with its feminine language – calling God the Holy Spirit 'she'! But that should not be a surprise because, as we know, the Hebrew word for spirit, *ruach*, is feminine. But I like the prayer more because it uses the language of hiddenness. The Spirit, we are told, 'comes along secret paths' and 'hides behind coincidence'. These are two of the phrases which speak of the hidden nature of the Spirit. This language of hiddenness is also accompanied by a sense of not knowing, for we have the twice repeated phrase 'We do not understand.'

All this is good theology, but it is not popular theology. Much talk about the Spirit in the contemporary Church is not elliptical or 'slant' like this language. It is descriptive, or at least claims to be descriptive. It appears to know where and when the Spirit will arrive and what it will do when it arrives. People seem to know what God is up to. This popular view of the Spirit does not easily sit with a number of scriptural perspectives, especially the perspective where God is unseen and where the work of the Spirit is compared, by Jesus, with the wind, which nobody knows where it comes from or where it is going (John 3.8).

So in many ways this prayer is an acknowledgement, an act of admission that God's activity is beyond description and that the Spirit works in the interstices of life; God accompanies life and waits for her opportunities. Coincidences may not be coincidences; accidents may be accidents from our point of view but from the Spirit's perspective may be opportunities to enter into the arena of life and play a part. In other words this prayer is an acknowledgement that there is another force at work in the affairs of men and women, a force which is unseen, which we cannot describe, but which is leaning upon us from the other side, from God's side of things. When our life fragments or cracks, when things go awry, when great emotions – like joy and sorrow – arise, then the Spirit comes along with them, breaks through into our existence and reveals her power and her presence.

God's Spirit is not manipulative, does not change the course of events in a direct way, but works in the way that a lover works, by leaning upon us with love until something happens which makes us aware that she (or, indeed, he) is present and wants to come closer, wants to be involved with us. How do we come to know that somebody loves us? It is all done by means of signs, unspoken things, hints, hidden signals. Things happen and we can either interpret them simply as things that have happened, with no further meaning, or we can look carefully, open things up in our minds and discover their hidden meaning. Love comes upon us unawares, by secret paths, and declares herself in subtle ways which, when we realize they are there, are totally powerful, totally sustaining and life-giving, full of an overwhelming power from on high.

Saying this prayer prepares the heart for the spirit's arrival.

H eavenly King, Paraclete, Spirit of Truth, present in all places
and filling all things, Treasury of good and Choirmaster of
life: come and dwell within us, cleanse us from all stains and save
our souls.

Liturgy of St John Chrysostom

This is a prayer to say at Pentecost. I have chosen it for two particular reasons. The first is that it clearly reflects the biblical teaching
that the Spirit of God is poured out on all creation. Our preconcep-
tion is that the Spirit of God is poured out upon the Church, a much
more limited exercise. We automatically take this as our understanding of the gift of the Spirit because of the account of the giving of the
Spirit in the Acts of the Apostles, where the apostles speak in tongues
and are filled with the Holy Spirit. But this account, where it is said
that everybody heard the apostles speak as if in their own tongue, is
an account of a reversal of what happened at Babel, when God gave
people different languages. Pentecost is thus portrayed as the possibility of a return to the original unity of humankind which God
intended. So while this account shows the apostles as the recipients
of the Spirit, it only does so because the apostles are the focus for a
renewal of all things. The Church is not the exclusive recipient of the
Spirit of God, but the sign that the Spirit is poured out on all things.
The Church is the sacrament of a new creation, a reminder to all
that reconciliation and peace are what we are all made for.

But this prayer is even wider and larger than that, for it under-
stands that God's Spirit is already 'present in all places and filling
all things'. This is the reality which we do not have to wait for any
longer but which Pentecost celebrates. To my mind this makes the
Christian celebration of Pentecost a truly wonderful feast which
speaks of the inspiration which everybody and indeed everything
has been and is being given. Here the violinist, the poet, the cook,
the craftsman, the pilot, the tender lover, the worker in steel, the
computer geek, the florist, the cleaner, the painter and decorator,
anybody and everybody with a skill of some kind, can come and give
thanks for what they can do. Moreover, here all creation can bend
the knee and say thank you for the sap which rises within it. Hildegard
of Bingen called the Holy Spirit *veriditas* or 'greenness', the very sap

of God in the veins of creation. This is a truly important insight for it means that we can join with all creation, all people and all things, on this feast, and give praise for the life which courses through the veins of all things living. Knowing that this life is given us from God is a mercy, a consolation and also a spur to allow that life to flow where human beings have blocked and restricted it.

But the other reason why I have included this prayer is for the phrase it contains, 'Choirmaster of life'. This is a wonderful way of looking at the Spirit of God, for it sees the Spirit as the animator, the one who oversees and energizes all the different parts of the creation, enabling each part to make its contribution and to be heard when its tune should be played.

OTHER PRAYERS

Bring us, O Lord, at our last awakening
into the house and gate of heaven,
to enter into that gate and dwell in that house
where shall be no darkness nor dazzling, but one equal
 light;
no noise nor silence, but one equal music;
no fears nor hopes, but one equal possession;
no ends nor beginnings, but one equal eternity
in the habitations of your glory and dominion,
world without end. Amen.

John Donne, 1573–1631

I love this prayer and often used it at funerals or memorial services. It is the sort of prayer which I wanted to use at the end of a busy day, during cathedral evensong, just as the light is slanting across the quire and there is that moment of pause as the business of the day is wrapped away into God. But it contains surprises.

When I am praying this prayer I think of John Donne himself, with his rackety life – his adventures on the high seas, his secret marriage and disgrace, his ambition and his eventual arrival at the Deanery of St Paul's. All this reminds me that he was like many modern men and women with an enormous number of ups and downs and short careers in this and that or nothing.

So this prayer is remarkable. It's remarkable that John Donne could have written it – was it, I wonder, because he led a rackety life that he could see through to the beauty and serenity of the life of God in such a way? Perhaps we would believe more intensely if our lives had more ups and downs? Perhaps rackety people have got more to offer us than we recognize? But the prayer is also remarkable because it speaks of the life of God as being somehow different to either extreme of human experience. God is not an excess of light, a dazzling, nor an excess of darkness. He is 'one equal light', a different kind of light entirely. Nor is he simply to be found in an excess of music, rather like a continuous hallelujah chorus, nor even, simply, in silence. There is a different quality about God, so well expressed by those repeated phrases, 'one equal music', 'one equal possession', 'one equal eternity'.

And I find that totally consoling. It mends all my fractures at the end of things. I know that my music often moves into unmusic, my light becomes darkness and then back again; but when all is said and done God's life is such that it will repair all that I might suffer.

God is not simply more of the same. He is not the height of ecstasy or even the end of ecstasy. He comes from a different place. He completes and transforms all that we lack and all that we have. He is a trumpet call from across the boundary.

G rant to us, O Lord, the royalty of inward happiness, and the
serenity which comes from living close to thee. Daily renew in
us the sense of joy, and let the eternal spirit of the Father dwell
in our souls and bodies, filling every corner of our hearts with light
and grace; so that, bearing about with us the infection of good
courage, we may be diffusers of life, and may meet all ills and cross
accidents with gallant and high hearted happiness, giving thee thanks
always for all things.

Robert Louis Stevenson, 1850–94

I love the language of this prayer. 'The royalty of inward happiness'
is a wonderful phrase. A 'royalty' is a sort of unearned reward,
and 'inward happiness', when it comes, does give you a sense of
being graced, being given something you did not earn or deserve,
and it fills you with dignity and life. And 'bearing about with us the
infection of good courage', is so right because 'good courage' is something which we can pass on to others just by being near them. The
word 'infection' saves us from being self-righteous, telling people
to be joyful all the time! I love it when I get to that line: 'meet all ills
and cross accidents with gallant and high hearted happiness'. 'Cross
accidents' are those which cross our path and give us the cross to
bear (as well as make us cross!), while that word 'gallant', so little
used nowadays, is such a great word to use about happiness – it
conveys the gallantry that happiness enables in us but also reminds
me at least of the topsails of a square-rigged sailing ship – one of
which is called the 'topgallant' and which when full of light and
wind carries the ship along with style and speed! It's a prayer in
which the language not only reflects the meaning but enhances it,
brings it alive, illustrates it, and fills you with the life it is talking
about as you read or speak it.

But I also love this prayer because it is about joy. Joy seems to
be in such short supply and such a hard-won virtue. This prayer
contradicts that. It says that you can be carried about by joy in
everyday life. This is not the way we usually see things. We think of
joy as having to be earned or achieved in some way or at least we
think that joy is not our normal condition. In this prayer Robert
Louis Stevenson is totally clear that joy is readily available and given

to us. It actually fills us with light so that we can 'infect' everything we do and everybody we meet with the same joy. The prayer implies that joy is there but we have forgotten about it somehow, lost it by our preoccupation with overcoming things ourselves. Joy is there, ready for us, and we have to open ourselves to it and let it fill our lives.

But there's another thing the prayer is saying. It recognizes that our lives are random and chancy. All sorts of things can and do happen, many of them quite unwelcome. But the point is not that joy is something we then have to summon up to counteract these 'cross accidents', but that joy is part of what is happening to us, essentially part of what we are given in everyday life. We can be joyful almost because everything is chancy and full of play. Treating whatever comes not as an obstacle but as a gift is joy. Life is not against us, this prayer says, rather all life, all creation, our whole existence, is full of the joy we think we have to obtain elsewhere.

L ord Christ,
help us to have the courage and humility to name our
   burdens
and lay them down
so that we are light to walk across the water
to where you beckon us.

Our pride,
armouring us,
hardening us,
making us defend our dignity by belittling others.

We name it and we lay it down.

The memory of hurts and insults,
driving us to lash out,
to strike back.

We name it . . .

Our antagonism against those
whose actions, differences, presence,
threaten our comfort or security.

We name it . . .

We do not need these burdens,
but we have grown used to carrying them,
have forgotten what it is like to be light.

Beckon us to lightness of being,
for you show us it is not unbearable.
Only so can we close the distance.
Only so can we walk upon the water.

Blessed are you, Lord Christ, who makest heavy burdens
   light.

Kathy Galloway (Iona Community)

Do you remember the novel *The Unbearable Lightness of Being* by the Czech writer Milan Kundera? Kundera was somebody who wanted to challenge the heavy hand of communism in his country by a mixture of laughter, mockery and fantasy. He thought this would work better than heavy political opposition, which in fact made communism more important than it was. This approach to communism puts me in mind of what one of my teachers at theological college used to say, that John the Baptist came into the world dressed in skins like any good prophet and saying 'Repent!', while Jesus came, turning cartwheels and saying something like 'Come off it . . .'. He could have added, 'Don't take yourself so seriously.'

This prayer reminds me of that. It is, properly speaking, a prayer that Christians would not take themselves and their burdens so seriously. Jesus' criticism of the Pharisees was just that, a plea not to take themselves and their religion too seriously. 'Lighten up,' he might have said in modern English. Like the Pharisees of whom Jesus spoke, we are in danger of making our act of repentance so important that grace doesn't have a chance of reaching us for all the heavy repenting that's going on! People do become obsessed with their own sin and talk endlessly about their problems so that they are actually never free of them because they are always talking about how they might be free of them. This is an obsessional self preoccupation, and only a good dose of ridicule or laughter can cure us. Although it must be said that there are some who are actually so ill that laughter is no cure – it only makes things worse.

Grace is a form of lightness of being which refuses to take itself seriously – indeed refuses to consider 'self' at all, because to do so means that self gets in the way. I actually think that this is what some of the mystics were talking about, and I was glad to have my view confirmed by Denys Turner, the Norris Hulse Professor of Theology at Cambridge, a noted scholar of mysticism. He makes the point that the mystics were not so much concerned with finding a way to God through experiences of personal union, but with criticizing the way in which preoccupation with spiritual experiences prevented you from allowing God to exercise his total freedom in you.* Looked at in this way mysticism is not for the few but for all of us because it

* See his book *The Darkness of God*, Cambridge University Press paperback.

is a sort of lightness of being, a total freedom, where we stop thinking about the importance of having a mystical experience at all!

That might be unbearable, which is why we reject mysticism in the Church today.

How great are the needs of your creatures on this earth, O God. They sit there, talking quietly and quite unsuspecting, and suddenly their need erupts in all its nakedness. Then, there they are, bundles of human misery, desperate and unable to face life. And that's when my task begins. It is not enough simply to proclaim you, God, to commend you to the hearts of others. One must also clear the path towards you in them, God, and to do that one must be a keen judge of the human soul . . . I embark on a slow voyage of exploration with everyone who comes to me.

And I thank you for the great gift of being able to read people. Sometimes they seem to me like houses with open doors. I walk in and roam through passages and rooms, and every house is furnished a little differently and yet they are all of them the same and every one must be turned into a dwelling dedicated to you, O God. And I promise you, yes I promise that I shall try to find a dwelling and a refuge for you in as many houses as possible. There are so many empty houses, and I shall prepare them all for you, the most honoured lodger. Please forgive this poor metaphor.

> Etty Hillesum, 1914–43 (from *An Interrupted Life:*
> *The Diaries of Etty Hillesum 1941–43*)

———◆———

We have all heard of Anne Frank, the little Jewish girl who wrote her diary in a secret attic in Amsterdam during the Nazi occupation. Not so many know of Etty Hillesum, another Jewish woman, somewhat older than Anne Frank but still in her twenties, who was writing a diary a few streets away. Etty was a young Jewish intellectual, an intimate friend of a therapist and a student of Russian. As the Nazis intensified their occupation of Holland and anti-Jewish laws were passed, Etty was found a job as a typist with the Jewish Council – the body set up by the occupation forces to represent Jewish interests. Jews were being moved to a transit camp outside Amsterdam, called Westerbork, and Etty decided to move there to work. She wanted to be near her people and bring them succour. This overwhelming prayer comes from the time when she was working in this camp trying to help those who were on their way to the death camps. Etty refused to leave or to hide, and in September 1943 she and her parents were placed on a transport to Auschwitz, where they perished. She threw a postcard out of the train as it left Holland. It was found by farmers, and on it was written, 'We left the camp singing'.

During her time in Westerbork Etty read the Bible, including the New Testament, as well as much else, especially her favourite poet, Rilke. This prayer is full of biblical imagery – 'dwelling', 'refuge', 'open doors'. What moves me about it is the absolute compassion it exhibits. Here is a young woman, whose diary in its early pages shows her to be confused about life and love, taking what she can where she can, but now, a sudden and overwhelming maturity develops and she is totally centred upon others. Not only that, in a strange way it is totally incarnational. It is not enough just to speak to people about you, she tells God, I must prepare a way in them for you. And here of course there are echoes of Isaiah. I must, she says, see people as rooms being made ready for that most honoured lodger who will come and dwell, and remain within them. And so in one sentence we move effortlessly from Isaiah to St John's Gospel.

How anybody could maintain this profound sense of the indwelling nature of God in the conditions of a wartime concentration camp is beyond me. It is an act of grace for which I, and countless others, both then and since, are profoundly grateful.

Etty's prayer is a lesson to the contemporary Church. She shows the true way of evangelism: the way of service, of involvement and the way of participation, sharing the lives of others to such an extent that she becomes the herald of God's innermost presence within us, even in the face of death. Would that more would learn from her.

I s not sight a jewel? Is not hearing a treasure? Is not speech a glory? O my Lord, pardon my ingratitude and pity my dullness who am not sensible of these gifts. The freedom of thy bounty hath deceived me. These things were too near to be considered. Thou presented me with thy blessings, and I was not aware. But now I give thanks and adore and praise thee for thine inestimable favours.

Thomas Traherne, 1636–74

This is the sort of prayer which cleanses your consciousness, which washes away your preoccupation with striving and the attempt to see and understand and gather to yourself things you think you need. It tells you that you have all you need if only you would refocus the inner eye of your consciousness and be aware of the simplicities of sight, hearing and speech. It's a prayer which reminds us of waking out of a deep sleep in which you have been grappling with apparently powerful forces to pull the curtains on bright light and a world refreshed by summer rain.

This, in fact, is the story of Thomas Traherne himself, a parish priest near Hereford at the time of the Restoration. Traherne had worked his way through a very Puritan education and was made the minister at Credenhill during the Cromwellian period, but his extensive reading of the early church fathers, particularly Gregory Nazianzus, and his personal journey took him into a profound recognition of the God-given nature of the created world. In the third of his *Centuries* he talks about this personal journey and how at one time he was 'swallowed up in the miserable gulf of idle talk and worthless vanities. I lived among dreams and shadows, like a prodigal son feeding upon husks with swine' (3.14).

But then on moving to the country he comes to himself and resolves to spend all of his time in search of what he calls 'felicity' and to be guided by 'an implicit faith in God's goodness'. So he wakes from sleep and rejoices in the beauty and life of common things.

So this prayer encapsulates his journey and ours, it brings us back to ourselves and to the beauty of what is already given. Traherne speaks to a frenzied age such as ours of the importance of happiness – what he calls 'felicity'.

This is a challenge to a Church which is preoccupied with change, evangelism and other forms of activism which simply mirror rather than challenge the spirit of the age. It is also a challenge to our psyches and the frenzied activity which we think they need in order to be alive. We are already alive, already blessed. The risk is we will not see it.

So the prayer reminds us that the spiritual life is really about stripping away what we do not need. Going to church and saying our prayers should bring us to that point where we laugh and weep at our own foolishness at the same time: weep because we have missed so much by looking in a far country for what we thought we needed, and laugh because, at last, we have come home to what God has given us and waited a long time for us to recognize and enjoy.

O God,
Enlarge my heart that it may be big enough to receive
the greatness of your love.
Stretch my heart
that it may take into it all those who with me around the
world believe in Jesus Christ.
Stretch it
that it may take into it all those who do not know him, but
are my responsibility because I know him.
And stretch it
that it may take in all those who are not lovely in my eyes,
and whose hands I do not want to touch;
through Jesus Christ, my saviour.

Prayer of an African Christian

I pray this prayer because it speaks to me of what has needed to
happen to me and, I hope, to some extent has happened and I want
to happen more, that my heart be enlarged. I also pray it because it
is a prayer by an unknown African Christian, and I spent four years
of my life in Africa and that experience enlarged my heart no end.

One experience which stretched my heart was that of visiting
missionaries who lived for years among the poorest of the poor,
often in the remotest regions. One of my colleagues had a small
private aeroplane, and he would take me up-country on trips,
visiting people whom he knew, taking fresh food or letters to them
in their rural fastnesses. On one such trip we landed close to the
Ethiopian border and met a group of priests and sisters who were
working with the people there. They had decided to give their lives
to this work and seldom, if ever, returned home to Europe. They
were not fanatics of any kind but had found fulfilment in living and
working with people who needed them. I knew that if I were to even
begin to think about such a way of life I would have to have a heart
far, far larger than the one I had. Just being there with them for the
day opened my heart and my eyes to what human beings are capable
of becoming.

In the Prologue to his Rule for monks, St Benedict, in the sixth
century, writes that he is proposing to establish a school of the Lord's

service. This rule, he says, may include a degree of restraint which might bring fear to those who find it difficult. This should not be the case, says Benedict, 'On the contrary, through the continual practice of monastic observance and the life of faith, our hearts are opened wide, and the way of God's commandments is run in a sweetness of love that is beyond words.'

My experience is that this is true, and while some might need a monastic community within which their hearts are enlarged, most of us have to make do with the monastery of life. Indeed, this monastery's demands are often sharp enough. But this is the way of the Lord's service we must follow, not the way of correct belief – although that will come – nor the way of telling others what correct belief entails – although that might well be needed; but first of all the way of larger hearts. We need to pray that our hearts are enlarged to accept those whom we find difficult to love, those we cannot abide, those whose views and lifestyle are not our own.

I do not work in Africa any longer; but, until recently, I worked in a cathedral. These vast and amazing buildings are constantly full of tourists, constantly being used for big services, for great occasions, for large-scale concerts. All sorts of people come through the doors making all manner of demands upon cathedral staff. Meanwhile the community which runs a cathedral is small and constant. The staff pray together daily, they worship and talk and argue together so that the good news is seen and heard by those who come. All this needs large hearts. While at the cathedral I was deeply thankful for my years in Africa which prepared me for this ministry and constantly prayed that my heart would be large enough to welcome those who came my way each day.

In this way I could be a sign of Christ's good news, which is at least as important as telling people about it.

O Lord of the lovers of mankind, who, for your sake, break the alabaster box of life, quicken your Church today with the ardour of the saints, so that by prayer and scholarship, by discipline and sacrifice, your name may be made truly known.

Kenneth Cragg

————◆◆◆————

The alabaster box in this prayer is, of course, a reference to the alabaster jar of very costly ointment which a woman pours over Jesus in the Gospels (see Mark 14.5 and parallels). In the Gospels the ointment is poured either over Jesus' head or his feet in prefiguration of his burial and as a symbol of his kingship. In this prayer the focus is subtly altered so that the alabaster jar becomes a box, and it symbolizes the life of the world which is broken open by ministers of the Gospel. Here the ministers of the Gospel, called 'lovers of mankind', take the place of the woman and break open our lives so that the healing and anointing life of God may fill the world. It is a beautiful simile, a striking reminder of the purpose of ministry in the Church.

This simile is then reinforced with three other phrases. The Church must be quickened 'with the ardour of the saints', and Christ's ministers must be people of 'prayer and scholarship', 'discipline and sacrifice' – the final note of sacrifice picking up again the echoes of the story of the woman's sacrifice of the ointment on Jesus just before his crucifixion.

There are several things to reflect upon here. The first is that the minister is a lover. The woman who poured the ointment over Jesus loved him. The disciples saw this as a waste, an act of foolish love. Whatever professional standards of ministry are called for in today's Church, nothing should be allowed to disguise the fact that the ministry is an act of foolish love by people whose model is an unknown woman in the Gospels who pours out her devotion upon the man Jesus.

Second, the task of the minister is, like the woman, to break open the mystery of life. Ministers have to know that there is a mystery hidden in the box of life and it is their task to release that so that God's presence is known and celebrated. His presence will then fill our lives just as the fragrance of the ointment filled the house. It is for the minister to find ways of acting and speaking so that this mystery, ultimately from God, is revealed. They have to open people's eyes to what they would not otherwise see.

Then there is mention of the means by which this may be done – 'prayer and scholarship, discipline and sacrifice'. These are not usual understandings, and very often they are lost in the welter of activity and business that overtakes the everyday working life of a parish priest. How refreshing it is when we meet a priest who is a real person of prayer and even more when one meets somebody who studies well and can make a real contribution to our thinking in a particular area, who can make us think again about something. And how often do we meet ministers who are prepared to accept gladly the limitations that their life will bring?

When we pray for the ministry of the Church we should not just pray for an increase in its numbers or for more leaders, but for more lovers and that these lovers of humankind should embrace a way of life which opens people's hearts and minds to mystery and does this gladly and joyfully.

We often used this prayer in the cathedral, usually when a new priest was being installed for work there. Some of them were deans or canons, some of them were receiving honorary positions in the cathedral after long service in the diocese, some were accepting a position of service in the everyday life of a great cathedral. These occasions were always done with a degree of ceremony and slow beauty as the bishop entered the quire and music and incense filled our senses. But whatever position they held, however important or however lowly, they were reminded by this prayer of the secret purposes of God for the ministry of the Church throughout the world.

God, we believe that you have called us together
to broaden our experience of you and of each other.
We believe that we have been called
to help in healing the many wounds of society
and in reconciling man to man and man to God.
Help us, as individuals or together,
to work, in love, for peace, and never to lose heart.
We commit ourselves to each other –
in joy and in sorrow.
We commit ourselves to all who share our belief in
  reconciliation –
to support and stand by them.
We commit ourselves to the way of peace –
in thought and deed.
We commit ourselves to you –
as our guide and friend.

Corrymeela Community, Ireland

Some years ago I went to the Corrymeela Community on a short visit. The Corrymeela Community is not a religious community in the generally accepted sense of that term. The members do not live together in one place. They are all people from different walks of life who have committed themselves to the work of reconciliation. They are engaged in different kinds of work in different parts of Northern Ireland, but their principal work is centred on the Antrim coast not far from the geological feature known as 'The Devil's Causeway'. There the community members bring together people from different denominations in the churches of Northern Ireland, particularly children from Protestant and Catholic communities. They live together for a week or so and learn at first hand about each other, learning about each other's prejudices and attempting to unravel the long and painful mistrust that inhabits that province.

We thought all this was wonderful until we found that we were also part of this process. 'Well,' said one little schoolgirl, looking quizzically at us folk from the English mainland, 'Well, do you think we over here are Irish or British?' Almost all of us instinctively answered 'Irish, of course,' thinking that was true because we had travelled across the water and were hearing English spoken with a certain accent. I must admit I also thought the little girls would be pleased that we thought them Irish; after all, I thought, I am usually pleased and proud to be English. But we met with cries of 'No, that's what everybody says. No, we are British.'

And a little thought made us realize that we had run into one of our own prejudices. The girls concerned were Protestants who were desperately trying to cling on to their British identity. They had no wish to be assimilated into a greater Ireland and certainly no wish to belong to Eire, the Irish Republic, where, of course, the majority of people are Roman Catholic. We had simply not understood the passion that such people have for their British identity.

So we learned that the quest for reconciliation is not simply something which others have to undergo, it is something in which all of us must be involved even when we do not think we need it. This is because there is a need for our hidden prejudices to be brought to the light of day and gently, but firmly, burned away in the light of God's love.

This prayer asks that we be given grace to broaden our experience of each other and of God. If God answers this prayer then he will certainly also ask us to broaden our experience of the hidden places of our hearts and empty them of prejudice. If we do not do that then we cannot really be said to be working for peace and reconciliation and, moreover, others will not join us on the common quest because they will only be too aware of our need for conversion.

As Jesus said, 'First take the plank out of your own eye . . .'.

O Lord Jesus Christ, draw thou our hearts unto thee; join them together in inseparable love, that we may abide in thee and thou in us, and that the everlasting covenant between us may stand sure for ever. Let the fiery darts of thy love pierce through all our slothful members and inward powers, that we, being happily wounded, may so become whole and sound. Let us have no lover but thyself alone; let us seek no joy or comfort except in thee.

Miles Coverdale, 1488–1568

This is an unusual prayer. Its language is dense and deeply spiritual, and displays an unusual capacity for rich and complex imagery. It uses the language of the mystical tradition of the Church, but comes from the pen of one who lived as this tradition appeared to be drawing to an end: he was, of course, very much part of the Reformation of the Church and, in his later years, a Puritan. Coverdale began religious life as an Augustinian Friar, and then would have learned something of the spirit of devotion which these lines contain.

The language of this prayer is deeply scriptural. 'Abiding', 'the everlasting covenant' and 'fiery darts' are all scriptural terms, while the lover and the beloved and the implied ravishment is straight from the Song of Songs. This is certainly to be expected from somebody who plainly loved the scriptures and whose translation of the scriptures into English deeply influenced the language of the Authorized Version. Coverdale's translation of the Psalter is embedded in the Book of Common Prayer and so still fills our minds with its richness.

The important point, however, is that Coverdale's language shows us how the mystical tradition of the Church, which is so much part of this prayer, is deeply scriptural. Many people still feel that the Christian mystical tradition uses concepts or imagery which come from outside of the Christian tradition, perhaps from eastern or Greek thought patterns, and so tend to think that the mystical way is not as 'Christian' as it ought to be. Perhaps they feel that mysticism smacks of inactivity or over-concentration on the interior life rather than the need for action in the world by committed people seeking the righteousness of the kingdom. These are false distinctions, for the tradition in which Coverdale was brought up was deeply scriptural and shows how the scriptures themselves feed the deep places of our souls and then release them in the freedom of the love of God to be for others. More and more the contemporary world is coming to know that the imagery of the mystical way relates to a 'postmodern' self-understanding. Coverdale's use of the phrase 'happily wounded' illustrates this. He writes, asking that we who are 'happily wounded, may become whole and sound'. This bears comparison with some words of Mechtild of Magdeburg, a Beguine of the thirteenth century, who said,

> Whosoever shall be sore wounded by love
> Will never become whole
> Save he embrace the self-same love
> Which wounded him

And, of course, Julian of Norwich, who died some sixty or seventy years before Coverdale was born, similarly develops the imagery of 'woundedness' in her *Showings*. This medieval emphasis on 'woundedness' is sometimes difficult for modern people to understand, but acceptance of the permanently wounded or 'open' nature of the self is, in much contemporary theology, a prerequisite of life lived in freedom with and through others. It is 'closure' of the wound which, according to many thinkers, especially for example the French thinker René Girard, brings difficulty and disaster to our lives and to the modern world.

So the prayer is deeply contemporary because so traditional. It asks us to leave our souls open to being wounded, that we may live in a permanent flow of love between us and others, and so too between us and the wounded Son of Man, Jesus.

Lord, thou art in me and shalt never be lost out of me, but I am not near thee till I have found thee. Nowhere need I run to seek thee, but within me where already thou art. Thou art the treasure hidden within me: draw me therefore to thee that I may find thee and serve and possess thee for ever.

Walter Hilton, fourteenth century (adapted)

This prayer addresses one of the great conundrums – theologians call them paradoxes – of the Christian faith, namely the dual experience of the proximity and absence of God. We know that God is beyond us and different and distant, or feels far away, simply because he is God. But we also know that he is 'in' us, nearer than breathing, closer than hands and feet. So we do not have to go on a great journey to reach him, but simply open ourselves to him.

This conundrum is remarked upon by so many writers. There is, for example, the famous poem 'On news' by Thomas Traherne. In this poem the writer begins by talking about news from a foreign country.

> News from a foreign country came,
> As if my treasure and my wealth lay there . . .

He says this is a dream of childhood, a childish belief. Rather everything he needs is nearby.

> But little did the infant dream
> That all the treasures of the world were by;
> And that himself was so the cream
> And crown of all which round about did lie . . .

Similarly the poet Francis Thompson thinks of God as other and threatening in his poem 'The hound of heaven', until right at the end, after having fled from this apparently alien and threatening God, he realizes that the threat is within himself.

> Halts by me that footfall:
> Is my gloom, after all,
> Shade of his hand, outstretched caressingly?

These poems, along with the prayer by Walter Hilton, show how difficult it is to believe that God is near and unthreatening. Indeed, how difficult it is to believe that he is present to and within us in a mysterious sense, that he is included in us.

Walter Hilton lived at a time of enormous difficulty in England, with plague and civil disorder commonplace. Yet he, and his near-contemporary Julian of Norwich, knew of the centrality of grace and presence in their lives. Julian has a similar remarkable sense of the interior presence of Christ and writes,

> And then our good Lord opened my spiritual eye, and showed me my soul in the midst of my heart. I saw the soul as wide as if it were an endless citadel, and also as if it were a blessed kingdom, and from the state which I saw in it, I understood that it is a fine city. In the midst of that city sits our Lord Jesus, true God and true man, a handsome person and tall, highest bishop, most awesome king, most honourable lord . . . He sits there erect in the soul, in peace and rest, and he rules and guards heaven and earth and everything that is.

Such an understanding in our own times – in their way just as terrible as the fourteenth century in England – would sustain us and give us pause before we inflicted more harm on others, in whose souls Christ also sits, 'erect . . . in peace and rest'.

Y ou alone are unutterable,
   From the time that you created all things that can be
spoken of.
You alone are unknowable,
From the time you created all things that can be known.
All things cry out about you;
Those which speak, and those which cannot speak.
All things honour you;
Those which think and those which cannot think.
For there is one longing, one groaning, that all things have
   for you.

All things pray to you that comprehend your plan and offer
   you a silent hymn.
In you, the One, all things abide, and all things endlessly
   run to you who are the end of all.

Gregory of Nazianzus, 329–89

Gregory of Nazianzus was one of three Fathers of the early Church
who are known as the Cappadocian Fathers. The other two were
Basil the Great and Gregory of Nyssa. These three men stand at an
important juncture in the life of the Church. While we may look
back at them now as theologians, they were, first of all, pastors and
administrators. Basil was a monk while the other two were bishops
of the Church. This meant that their theology emerged from their
experience within the fellowship of the Church, an experience of
being in communion. Indeed, part of their struggle was against the
hierarchical authority of the emperor. This experience and this struggle enabled these men to speak about God in a more profound way.
They found they could not speak of him as other Christian theologians had done, using the terms of Greek philosophy, where God
and the world were essentially one; nor could they speak of him
using the Gnostic terminology so prevalent in the Mediterranean
world of the time, in which there is a great gulf fixed between God
and creation. This was where their experience of being in relationship within the Christian community came to their aid. They spoke
of God as essentially being in communion, where the being of God

is a relational being. Above all God exists in relationships, and centrally in the relationship of love. Nor can he exist before that relationship of love is established, as if the relationship of love were some sort of 'add-on' to his being. God has no true being apart from communion.

One enormously important consequence of this way of thinking about God is that it establishes the Trinity as central to the being of God. 'Trinity' is not something added on to God merely as a way of understanding or talking about him. It is how God is. It also means that everything that is derives its being from God and exists in relationship to him. The whole creation, animate and inanimate, human and non-human, is in communion with God as coming from him and returning to him. God's desire to create is central to him, and this desire is then placed in all things.

So you can see from this little bit of theology how this prayer has come about. It speaks of how all things are in relationship with God.

> All things cry out about you;
> Those which speak, and those which cannot speak.
> All things honour you;
> Those which think and those which cannot think.
> For there is one longing, one groaning, that all things have for you.

It also speaks of how all things pray to God. I find this a wonderful thought, and as I walk about the Somerset countryside I think of all that I see – trees, grass, birds – all calling out praise to God by simply existing as they are. The Fathers of the Church knew about this more than we, who look at the creation through the eyes of the scientific enlightenment and so see it as neutral rather than alive with praise. Prayer is what somebody called 'Primary Speech', the original language of the creation, the first, natural and uninhibited language of all things as they cry out to the one who gave them life and breath and so return that life and breath to him.

When the heart is hard and parched up, come upon me with a shower of mercy.

When grace is lost from life, come with a burst of song.

When tumultuous work raises its din on all sides shutting me out from beyond, come to me my Lord of silence, with thy peace and rest.

When my beggarly heart sits crouched, shut up in a corner, break open the door, my king and come with the ceremony of a king.

When desire blinds the mind with delusion and dust, O thou holy One, thou wakeful, come with thy light and thunder.

Rabindranath Tagore, 1861–1941

Rabindranath Tagore was a Hindu poet from Bengal who was part of the renaissance of Hindu thinking and writing which took place in India during the nineteenth and twentieth centuries. Tagore knew Gandhi and engaged in dialogue with him about the way forward for India. Both Tagore and Gandhi were very interested in Jesus Christ, and although neither became a Christian they were very influenced by Christian thinking.

I love reading this prayer and using it in my personal devotion. It recalls me to acknowledge my need for grace and the way grace bursts in upon my life when I have boxed myself into a corner of some kind. It can clearly be prayed by Christians, as the grace of which it speaks is the gift of the 'Lord' who is referred to several times. It employs beautiful imagery for grace – saying it is a shower of mercy, a burst of song, silence, regal ceremony and then light and thunder. In each of these images grace is understood as breaking open a closed mental and spiritual life. In each petition it is acknowledged that the soul has that fatal capacity to lock itself away, perhaps because of grief or sadness, perhaps because of selfishness, perhaps because I have locked myself away in some obsessive desire. The reasons why the soul locks itself away from life as gift are only hinted at, but all of us know how we are prone to this and are not always aware of what we are doing. So we need our gracious Lord to open us and return us from a land of delusion to the reality of life as gift.

Because the clear understanding of this prayer is that God's life comes in from elsewhere, both as gift but also as judgement, as cleansing and refining, as that which breaks down the enclosure of the ego self. The arrival of grace is understood as a form of release from a bondage or constriction that the soul has accepted. We all know times when we are 'hard and parched up', when grace is lost, when we are caught up in the fascination and tumult of work, when we are shut up in a corner, when we are blinded by our own desires, and here Tagore means not just sexual desires but all obsessive desires which take us away from our true selves. All this has to be broken down.

One word more. While we might well understand grace as a shower of rain or as silence or as light and thunder we might not so easily understand grace as 'ceremony'. In the cathedral where I used to work, ceremony is part of life. This is managed by the cathedral virgers, who lead the clergy about, slowly and quietly. They bow to the clergy, enabling the clergy to bow in return. A colleague once found this far too formal and asked that it be dispensed with or at least reduced. But reflection persuaded us that it should not be diminished, because it actually forced us to be gracious to each other and to ourselves. It encouraged us to walk slowly, when we had been hurrying all day, to catch our breath when we had been breathless all day, and to pay attention and give respect to other people. In this sense ceremony brings us back into ourselves and asks us to let go and be quiet and gracious. In that sense it is very powerful and really is the ceremony of a king.

O God, make the door of this house wide enough to receive all who need human love and fellowship; narrow enough to shut out all envy, pride and strife. Make its threshold smooth enough to be no stumbling block for children, nor to straying feet, but rugged and strong enough to turn back the tempter's power. God make the door of this house the gateway to thine eternal kingdom.

Thomas Ken, 1637–1711 (on St Stephen Walbrook Church, London)

This lovely prayer is just right to be placed at the entrance of any church. It was written by Thomas Ken, who was Bishop of Bath and Wells from 1685 to 1691. He is the nearest Wells has to a saint and is remembered as having practised generous hospitality in his Palace in Wells, where he would entertain twelve poor people from the town to lunch each Sunday. The table around which they sat is still in the palace, and this prayer of his is used daily in his cathedral during the visitor season. It has been adopted as the prayer of the Ministry of Welcome in the cathedral and is said each day by the chaplain on duty, who welcomes visitors as they gather at the medieval astronomical clock in the cathedral transept. After the clock has struck and the jousting knights have whirled around once more, the chaplain asks the visitors to be silent for a moment and uses this prayer.

Churches need to learn how to welcome people across their threshold. People are nervous as they cross thresholds, as I discovered when I was the director of a study and retreat centre. The point of welcome for people coming away to a different place is crucial, and difficulties or problems during their stay could often be traced back to an awkward arrival. People can often be seen hesitating outside of Wells Cathedral, wondering whether or not to go in. So welcoming people into a house of prayer needs to be sensitive and attentive. This also needs to be the case in our homes as well as in our churches. Hospitality to our homes is an act of grace, and opening our home to others reminds them and us of the gift that life really is.

But the most important 'opening' must be that of our hearts and lives. Faithful people are those who are always open to whatever comes in the confidence that nothing can unsettle the work of God within them. God has already 'come' and stands within them as 'the welcomer' or the quiet discerner of the truth and value of whatever comes. The person who is rooted in God in this way is able, because of his inner security, to quietly reject what is not from God and affirm what is. He or she stands at the door of life as it unfolds, quietly sure that all is well within. He or she has no need to oppose what is ungodly with a great deal of flash and show, as if winning the battle was all. The battle, in fact, has already been won. He or she can quietly go about their business confident in God and without looking to achieve further security or strength.

This was in fact the great virtue of Bishop Thomas Ken. He quietly opposed the King's liaison with Nell Gwynne, and risking the King's wrath, he actually won his deep respect. During the aftermath of the Monmouth Rebellion, when many were imprisoned in the cloisters of Wells Cathedral, he visited them and openly sought from the authorities greater clemency than Judge Jeffreys had been minded to exercise. And when William and Mary came to the throne he refused to take the oath of loyalty, as he believed that James was still the rightful king. He was deposed from his bishopric as a consequence and lived the rest of his life in simplicity at Longleat, refusing to be a cause of dissension or trouble. His quiet confidence in the interior love of God stood him in good stead during those days.

So praying this prayer is essentially an act of confidence in the Christ who has already come and who lives within us.

O God, we are one with you.
You have made us one with you.
You have taught us that if we are open to one another, you
dwell in us.
Help us to preserve this openness and to fight for it with all
our hearts.
Help us to realize that there can be no understanding where
there is mutual rejection.
O God, in accepting one another wholeheartedly, fully,
completely, we accept you, and we thank you, and we
adore you; and we love you with our whole being,
because our being is in your being,
our spirit is rooted in your Spirit.
Fill us then with love, and let us be bound together with
love as we go our diverse ways, united in this one Spirit
which makes you present in the world, and makes you
witness to the ultimate reality that is love.
Love has overcome.
Love is victorious.

Thomas Merton, 1915–68

This prayer springs out of a realization that the human person is
not, finally, separated from God. At root our spirit is somehow in
God. It is difficult for contemporary Christians who stand in a more
Protestant tradition to realize the truth of this. But this is a simple
evangelical truth to which both St John's Gospel and the words of
St Paul testify.

Perhaps the best way of understanding this is to use the biblical
image of the human person as a tree with roots which reach down to
the water of life and are fed by that living water. The image of the
vine, with the faithful being grafted onto the stock which is Christ, is
entirely similar.

What this prayer does is remind the one who prays it that this
ultimate rootedness in God and the spirit of God – a spirit which
waters our very roots – also roots us in other people. Openness to
our rootedness in God brings us into union with others, and openness to others brings us into union with God. Too often the unity

with God does not lead to a sense of unity with others. The relation-ship is understood to be entirely vertical; its depths have not been sufficiently explored.

Thomas Merton came to know of how his ultimate unity with God also brought him into a loving unity with others during his years in a silent Trappist monastery. He had been a rather dis-ordered undergraduate in Cambridge just before the Second World War, but then, after a conversion experience, entered the Trappist monastery of Gethsemani in Kentucky. After over twenty years in this silence he found himself in the local town of Louisville, where his diary records, with a touch of surprise, an experience of loving unity with others. He writes,

> In Louisville, at the corner of Fourth and Walnut, in the centre of the shopping district, I was suddenly overwhelmed with the realisation that I loved all those people, that they were mine and I theirs, that we could not be alien to one another even though we were total strangers. It was like waking from a dream of separateness, of spurious self-isolation in a special world, the world of renunciation and supposed holiness.

Religious people have to explore the depths of their relationship with God to find that it involves them in a relationship with others. It is also incumbent upon those who believe in the importance of loving and serving others, but who do not have any religious faith, to explore the depths of their relationship with others to find, deep within it, at its root, a relationship with the unknown God.

When we pray this prayer we should ask that all of us involved in relationships should explore them to the very depths and find the other, whether this be the otherness of God or the otherness of the other person, also there.

I learned that love was our Lord's meaning.
And I saw for certain, both here and elsewhere,
That before ever he made us, God loved us;
And that his love has never slackened, nor ever shall.
In this love all his works have been done,
And in this love he has made everything serve us;
And in this love our life is everlasting.
Our beginning was when we were made, but the love in which he
    made us never had beginning.
In it we have our beginning.
All this we shall see in God for ever.
May Jesus grant this.

Julian of Norwich, 1342–c.1416

Julian of Norwich has rightly become a very important figure in the life of the Church today, partly because she was a woman and wrote of the motherhood of God. While that remains important, Julian's thought is more complex, and she makes a profound contribution to the spiritual tradition of the Church in a number of other directions.

We might forget that she lived at a time of great social upheaval, when new ideas were struggling to be born but when the Church was apparently unwilling to countenance them. Lollardy, for instance, was condemned and its adherents burned in the Lollards' Pit not far from Julian's cell. The Church was more concerned about social control, while Julian's visions taught her that 'love was our Lord's meaning'. But this love was not simply an emotion, a feeling which should be expressed. It was the very constituent fabric of the universe. This was how things were. This was the reality. And so Julian came to see that there was no judgement in God.

> . . . we deserve pain, blame and wrath. And despite all this, I saw truly that our Lord was never angry, and never will be.

This is a remarkable statement for anybody in Julian's position to make and was deeply subversive of the teaching of the Church at the time, but Julian was what we might call 'a theological worrier' and worried away at what she thought was somehow not quite right. In

many ways her troubles and her visions were the result of theological worry of this kind, and the tension that this worry set up in her.

Another part of her worry was about the role of God the creator. She came to see, in her Third Revelation, that God was not just the creator, not just the sustainer, but the author of all things in the present. Though it might appear that men or the evil one is in control, in and through appearances God is doing everything and doing it well.

> See, I am God. See, I am in all things. See, I do all things. See, I never remove my hands from my works, nor ever shall without end. See, I guide all things to the end that I ordain them for, before time began, with the same power and wisdom and love with which I made them; how should anything be amiss?

This is part of her conclusion that love is the meaning of things and that in this love all of God's works have been done.

We should pray for a similar understanding in our own day in order that the Church should be a sign against the popular belief that things are in our hands and that we have to control them all. Perhaps, like Julian, we should worry more about received truths.

B lessed are you, Lord our God, King of the universe, who makes us holy through doing his commands, and delights in us. Willingly and with love he gives us his holy Sabbath to inherit, for it recalls the act of creation. This is the first day of holy gatherings, a reminder of the exodus from Egypt. Because you chose us to be holy among all peoples, willingly and with love you gave us your holy Sabbath to inherit. Blessed are you, Lord, who makes the Sabbath holy.

Jewish blessing for the Sabbath ('Kiddush')

I used to hear this prayer regularly when I worked as the director of a study centre devoted to reconciliation and peace. There we regularly held Jewish–Christian study weekends, and the Friday evening was, of course, the beginning of the Sabbath. When both Jews and Christians were assembled at the meal table the traditional Sabbath blessings were offered and the candles lit. Participants of the weekend would experience Jewish liturgies on the Saturday but Christian ones on the Sunday, and all this interspersed with study of both Hebrew and Christian scriptures. Each study group contained a Jewish and a Christian teacher. This way understanding and, hopefully, tolerance, was increased and differences explored and recognized.

When the lights were lit and we had all wished each other a peaceful Sabbath ('Shabbat Shalom') I always wondered why the Christian Sunday was so dry and serious by comparison. For Jews the Sabbath is a day of joy. Songs are sung, families meet, married couples make love, no work is done as this was the day on which God rested and took pleasure in the goodness of what he had made. Surely Sunday too was a celebration of the creation, certainly it was a celebration of liberation from death, when our Passover Lamb was sacrificed for us, so why had our celebration become so limited and churchy?

Plainly there are a number of reasons for this, but one of them must be the loss or neglect in Christian thinking of an understanding of creation as 'good'. If you were to ask a Jewish Rabbi and a Christian priest to preach on the first chapters of Genesis, the betting is that the Christian priest would spend a great deal of time showing how the Genesis account of the creation can or cannot be reconciled with the scientific understanding of evolution. The Rabbi on the other hand would almost certainly see this as an opportunity to remind his hearers of the goodness of creation and how this is celebrated each Sabbath. Christian thinking is still preoccupied with the apparent disjuncture between scientific and biblical accounts of creation, even though it should be plain to the simplest mind that they are quite different matters dealing with quite different issues. This preoccupation results in an impoverished understanding of the place of creation in our lives. It reduces creation to a conundrum. Jewish thinking, happily, jumps over all that straight into an ac-knowledgement of God's goodness, who, as the prayer says, 'delights in us'.

Thomas Merton, an American Trappist, spent some time reflect-ing on the creation, and he said,

> The doctrine of creation is not merely an answer to the question of how things got to be what they are by pointing to God as a cause. On the contrary, the doctrine of creation as we have it in the Bible . . . starts not from a question about being but from a direct intuition of the act of being.

He continues,

> My being is given me not simply as an arbitrary and inscrutable afflic-tion, but as a source of joy, growth, life, creativity and fulfilment.

Greater use by Christians of the Jewish Kiddush might help them to understand what Thomas Merton is saying.

O God, thou art peace. From thee is peace and unto thee is peace. Let us live, our Lord, in peace, and receive us in thy paradise, the abode of peace. Thine is the majesty and the praise. We hear and we obey. Grant us thy forgiveness, Lord, and unto thee be our becoming.

Prayer at the close of Salat

This prayer is said by Muslims at the close of Salat, the formal set prayers offered five times each day. It is hard for Christians to realize the centrality of these formal acts of prayer for the Muslim. A Christian child may be taught prayers by his mother or father, he may learn something of the fellowship of Christian worship, but have little knowledge, unless he or she decides to become a minister of the Church, of the official service books of the Church. In Islam the exact contrary is the case. A Muslim child is taught first the practice of the set prayers – Salat.

Constance Padwick, who was a scholar of Islamic worship and wrote a groundbreaking study of Islamic devotion in the 1930s, says,

> Salat, then, is the dominant note in the music of Moslem devotions. The rubrics commonly enjoin that the various devotions shall be said after the prayers of one of the canonical hours . . . To draw a comparison from Christendom, it is as though the whole laity of the Anglican Church had to say the offices of Morning and Evening Prayer daily throughout the year before it was permissible for them to say any other prayers.

This is in principle, for Christians, very similar to the monastic way, where the recitation of the divine office comes before anything else, whether this be work or private prayer. Such comparisons give Christians some idea of the power of Muslim devotion and of its place in the life of the Muslim community. This it is which links the believer to God in a form of spiritual contract, a deep submission before the presence of the Almighty. Moreover Salat is something offered by the community of which the individual Muslim is a part, so there is a further parallel with monastic practice here. Would it make for a stronger sense of faith and prayer if Christians were taught the rhythm and structure of daily prayer before the interior spiritual content? Would it help Muslims if they had a deeper sense of personal piety and regarded that as more important than adherence to outward practice? Merely asking these questions shows that both ways produce faithful believers.

All that apart, what this fine prayer does reveal is not only a sense of worship but also a deep sense of handing over of the self to God. God holds all things and forgives all things and in him all things come to be, for 'unto thee be our becoming'. This profound sense of abandonment to divine providence, which is equally found within the Christian tradition, is what brings peace to the soul. For the Muslim as for the Christian, 'All things work together for good for those who believe.'

O Jesus Christ, you knew the workshop of Joseph and you saw the sweat of the labourer. Bless those who work and those who employ workers. May your Church, the steward of your way of life, teach us how to labour honestly and how to reward work justly. Help us to uphold the dignity of human labour, that whether in physical or in mental work the person is more important than the job. Guide those who make decisions about employment and payment; temper our discussions about money and work with a sense that we are your servants, that we may be motivated neither by a greed for money nor by a desire to get as much as we can for as little pay as possible. May we seek the welfare of each other, remembering that we all have but one master, who is also our judge and our saviour, even the same Jesus Christ.

Ralston Smith, Jamaica

This is the sort of prayer that should have been written in London or New York rather than in Jamaica, for it is those financial capitals of the world that need justice in the workplace as much as the poor countries of the world. Decisions taken there affect vast numbers of people. But whether it is in large corporate bodies in our great cities or in small workshops in poor villages, the same need for justice and fair dealing is present. Too often our prayers focus on our relationship with God or Jesus, too often we are thinking of how we feel in prayer. The real need is to pray that our life and work should be just and equitable.

This was brought home to me this year when my wife and I went on a 'People to People Tour' of India organized by Traidcraft, the largest Fairtrade organization in the UK. Traidcraft supports the work of a large number of small enterprises across India where the workers are paid a fair wage and working conditions uphold the dignity of the worker. We visited a stonecutting workshop in Agra, a city where stonecutters have been at work since the building of the Taj Mahal. There we saw how simple matters such as fans to extract dust, masks to protect the lungs from dust, medicare and a fair wage do not have to be neglected in order to achieve a reasonable profit margin or steady production targets. We also visited a factory in Kerala devoted to the production of fruit juice and candied ginger which was owned by the four hundred or so small farmers in the region who grow the fruit. Most movingly we visited a woman's co-operative on the Ganges delta founded by a small group of women whose husbands could not or would not find work. They now work with thousands of women across the delta who grow silk worms and spin and weave their own silk. The silk is then dyed and printed with their own designs in vegetable dyes and sold to Traidcraft and other Fairtrade outlets in Calcutta and across the world. All of these groups were concerned with the quest for justice and equity in the workplace.

In one of the workshops a large board hung over the workers inscribed with a quotation from Gandhi which read,

> Poverty is not only about shortage of money. It is about rights and relationships, about how people are treated and how they regard themselves, about powerlessness, exclusion and loss of dignity. Yet the lack of an adequate income is at its heart . . .

This is what the prophets of the Hebrew Scriptures spoke of, and unless it is part of a renewed Christian life no personal conversion is really complete.

O living God, God of all the earth,
  send down the Spirit of your Son Jesus Christ;
heal our wounded hearts;
make peace in the place of conflict;
grant love in the face of revenge;
build hope where fear prevailed;
establish trust across our divisions.
Let the light of truth disperse the shadows,
and the dawn of justice banish hatred,
that our lives may be saved,
our land restored,
Africa set free
And the love of God be known in joy for all.

Bishop Peter Lee, South Africa
(known as 'The Sharpeville Prayer')

South Africa is the most beautiful land. I spent a short time there two or three years ago speaking at conferences of Anglican clergy, many of them working in the townships of Cape Province. I was most moved by their belief that peace could come in the place of conflict and by their capacity to live the gospel in the midst of so much poverty and all that accompanies it.

During our stay we lodged with a small group of retired clergy. One evening one of them asked if early the next morning my wife and I might like to accompany him to the local church, where they prepared food and drink for unemployed men and then distributed it to them at various points in the city. We rose early and spent some time preparing mounds of peanut butter sandwiches and making sweet tea which was then loaded into cars and taken to a number of crossroads downtown where unemployed men waited to see if they would be taken on for the day, mostly by the building industry, which would send lorries to pick them up if needed. There was a large crowd of men where we went, but plainly no work.

We asked the men – who were used to this routine as the church concerned had been organizing this food run for many years – to form an orderly queue. Our leader then asked whether they wished to give thanks for the food. One of them stepped forward and they all, in unison, raised their hats from their heads, and held them in the air above their heads while the prayer was said in Xhosa, with its clicks resounding in the morning air. I was somewhat surprised but moved by this corporate witness, but also by their gentleness and gratitude, for one peanut butter sandwich and a cup or two of tea were precious little, and I was told they would not have much else to eat that day.

These men and I were miles apart, but even in the most terrible poverty this separation could be overcome for a moment. That moment was no more than a sign of possibilities, a sign that we could meet across the terrible gulf between us; but, I reflected, human beings need not lose their dignity and so their capacity for reconciliation. That capacity, what the ancients called *capax dei*, our ability to make room for God, is inherently present. Once that is recognized, then we can begin to move towards each other, and 'make peace in the place of conflict; grant love in the face of revenge; build hope where fear prevailed; establish trust across our divisions'.

O God, who by thy Spirit in our hearts dost lead men and women to desire thy perfection, to seek for truths and to rejoice in beauty, illuminate and inspire we beseech thee, all thinkers, writers, artists and craftsmen; that, in whatsoever is true and pure and lovely, thy name may be hallowed and thy kingdom come on earth; through Jesus Christ our Lord.

Prayer (slightly adapted) found in St Anselm's Chapel,
Canterbury Cathedral

Anselm was, of course, one of two Archbishops of Canterbury (the other being Lanfranc) to come from the Abbey of Bec in northern France in the Middle Ages. Anselm was an Italian, from Aosta, and became Abbot of Bec before being called by William II to be Archbishop of Canterbury in 1093.

As well as being involved in some of the most difficult arguments between the kings of England and the Papacy, Anselm was himself a thinker and a writer, actually one of the most important scholars between the early Church and the high Middle Ages. He it was who was responsible for what is known as the Ontological Argument for the existence of God. His treatise on the atonement, how men and women are saved (*Cur Deus Homo*), is still read and commented upon as one of the classical texts of Christian thinking.

So it is appropriate that this prayer is to be found in the chapel dedicated to him in Canterbury, and that it not only reminds us of Anselm the scholar but also celebrates the work of craftsmen and artists. The basilica consecrated by Augustine at Canterbury had been destroyed by fire in 1067, but the church was still being rebuilt in Anselm's day, so the scholar and the craftsmen lived and worked together.

Thanksgiving for and celebration of 'thinkers, writers, artists and craftsmen' is an essential part of the Church's witness to the beauty and difference of God. A neglect of such people by the Church is tantamount to a neglect of the beautiful and its capacity to hint at the existence of the one who is the source of beauty. Such neglect is not only a neglect of the truth, it is also a neglect of people's deepest longings and brings the Church into disrepute with those who know the power of the beautiful. Bishop Richard Harries says,

Unless the Christian faith has an understanding and place for the arts it will inevitably fail to win the allegiance of those for whom they are the most important aspect of life . . . Unless the experience of beauty in nature and the arts is encompassed and affirmed the Christian faith will seem to have nothing of interest or importance to say.

'Thinkers, writers, artists and craftsmen' are profoundly aware that we all have a desire for God placed in us by the Spirit of God. Giving that desire free rein to push at the edges of received forms of expression, looking for ways in which the truth of God can be made known afresh in each generation, should not be a difficulty for any of us.

This prayer celebrates the existence of such a desire. Saying it opens your life to its activity.

Yﾞou keep us waiting . . . you, the God of all time, want us
to wait
For the right time in which to discover
Who we are, where we must go,
Who will be with us, and what we must do.

So thank you . . . for the waiting time.

You keep us looking . . . you, the God of all space,
Want us to look in the right and wrong places for signs of
hope,
For people who are hopeless,
For visions of a better world which will appear
Among the disappointments of the world we know.

So thank you . . . for the looking time.

You keep us loving . . . you, the God whose name is love,
Want us to be like you –
To love the loveless and the unlovely and the unlovable;
To love without jealousy or design or threat;
And, most difficult of all, to love ourselves.

So thank you . . . for the loving time.

And in all this, you keep us.
Through hard questions with no easy answers;
Through failing where we had hoped to succeed
And making an impact when we felt we were useless;
Through the patience and the dreams and the love of others,
And through Jesus Christ and his Spirit, you keep us.

So thank you . . . for the keeping time,
And for now,
And for ever,
Amen.

By John L. Bell © WGRG, Iona Community, G2 3DH

A friend of mine sent me this prayer when she heard that I was compiling a book of favourite prayers. She wrote to me saying,

> I enclose a prayer that I used time and again for months and years after John had died when the days were dark and the way ahead un-clear and I couldn't pray as I had before. It was a time when I was questioning God as well as my life. The prayer acted as some sort of anchor rope in deep and stormy water. Picture God as the anchor – deep in the dark; out of sight but somehow – tenuously (!) – keeping me steady . . . holding me but not very well! I was like a little boat on the surface – tossed about and shipping water. Tussling with the connection. It was a prayer for that time and so was important to me for that.

I have included the prayer because what Vanda experienced is what so many people experience, and sharing what she says and the prayer that she found so helpful after the death of her partner may help others. But I've also included it because I think that during this dark time she discovered something which is so important in our spiritual life, namely the realization that the whole Christian life is actually a life of looking, waiting, loving and keeping. It is not just during dark times that we have to remember that our faith is one where we keep on looking and waiting and loving through all of the difficulties, accepting them and living with them even though they are unresolved, and apparently irresolvable, but that the whole of our faithful life will be like this.

Too much Christianity these days claims to be a set of answers, the truth for people who apparently do not know. Friends persuade me, somewhat reluctantly, that this is a helpful 'way in' for many people, and that so many people have been helped by this approach to come to a deeper faith. My problem is that such a way in remains the end as well as the beginning and that there is little encourage-ment for people to move on to a more mature faith, one which does not require 'answers' but is content, or even not content, to struggle and to look and to keep on looking.

God is more of a reality in whose reality we share than a truth which we can pick up and put in our pocket. Sometimes it is only dark days that reveal that to us.

Trust in God
Let nothing disturb you,
Let nothing frighten you;
All things pass:
God never changes.
Patience achieves
All it strives for.
He who has God
Finds he lacks nothing,
God alone suffices.

Teresa of Avila, 1515–82 (her bookmark)

I think if I had been Teresa of Avila I would have been glad of this prayer as my bookmark and daily reminder. Her life was not an easy one. She came from a family of 'conversos', those who had converted from Judaism at the time of the expulsion of Jews and Muslims from Spain in the 1490s. She was subject to harassment by the Inquisition for her personal religion. She suffered from the antagonism of many and yet established convents all over Spain and wrote so much that has become part of the Christian tradition. Living as she did at a time of enormous civil and religious conflict, and being, as she was, at the heart of the reformation of the Church, she needed a prayer such as this.

She was plainly a strong woman. Her strength of character certainly came from her upbringing and was sharpened by experience, but it also came from her understanding of God. For Teresa there is a deep well of life which constantly springs up in the heart of the believer. This she came to rely upon totally. She writes about it in *The Interior Castle*, where she uses the imagery of water. As those of you who have visited Andalucia will know, water plays an important part in the Moorish gardens with which Teresa would have been familiar. She imagines two troughs of water which are filled in different ways: one where the water comes from a great distance 'through many aqueducts and the use of much ingenuity'; in the other where the water rises from deep within the trough itself, from an interior spring. Teresa compares these two troughs to two ways of prayer: the first uses many aids to prayer and meditation and so makes a great deal of noise, but in the other 'the water comes from its own source, which is God'. This form of prayer is a gift. She says,

> It seems that since that heavenly water begins to rise from this spring I'm mentioning that is deep within us, it swells and expands our whole interior being producing ineffable blessings; nor does the soul even understand what is given to it there.

In St John's Gospel Jesus says,

> Let anyone who is thirsty come to me, and let the one who believes in me drink. As the scripture has said, 'Out of the believer's heart shall flow rivers of living water.'   (John 7.37)

Teresa's capacity to do what she did came from an inner awareness of the life of God constantly given to her. This was the difference between her and her detractors, who found it difficult to credit a woman, a *converso* woman at that, with spiritual credibility.

Perhaps the times are not that different now, and so her bookmark can still serve a similar purpose for today's women and men.

O Holy Spirit,
  Give me faith that will protect me
from despair, from passions and from vice;
Give me such love for God and men
as will blot out all hatred and bitterness;
Give me hope that will deliver me
from fear and faintheartedness.

> Dietrich Bonhoeffer (prayed as he awaited trial for
> his part in a plot against Hitler)

I have a personal debt to Bonhoeffer. Immediately after my final undergraduate examinations I read his book *The Cost of Discipleship*, a moving exposition of the Beatitudes and the Sermon on the Mount in which Bonhoeffer takes the Church to task for settling for 'cheap grace' rather than the 'costly grace' of which Jesus speaks. Of course Bonhoeffer himself was called to bear the ultimate cost of discipleship when he faced death at the hands of the Nazis, but it was reading his book that confirmed me in my decision to be ordained. There were, of course, other influences besides that of Bonhoeffer, but he was an inspiration.

I think we have little understanding of the importance of Bonhoeffer in the English Church. We see him, rightly, as a martyr, and this he was, but he became caught up in the struggle against Hitler for theological reasons which are, in the end, his proper legacy to the Church today. He believed that the Church had lost sight of its role as a witness to society. Bonhoeffer's great study *Ethik* (some of which was confiscated by the Gestapo, some of which was hidden when Bonhoeffer was arrested) drew him to the conclusion that the quest for the Kingdom of God should not remain within the personal and spiritual realm but should involve the whole of our social existence. The State was not free from answering theological claims. This was a distinct shift in Lutheran thinking and, of course, brought Bonhoeffer onto a collision course with the State. The State's view was that religion was for the interior life and could not impinge on State matters. It was, of course, the acceptance of such circumstances which had prevented many German Christians from seeing and speaking about the Nazi treatment of the Jews in the years before the war. Bonhoeffer's thinking led him and a number of other Lutheran pastors to form the 'Confessing Church' after the historic 'Barmen Declaration', and Bonhoeffer became responsible for the training of pastors for this Church in a secluded seminary in the Black Forest until it was closed by the authorities. In setting up this seminary he travelled to England to see how the Church of England did these things, and he was much influenced by the quasi-monastic seminaries then in existence and the disciplined life which they aimed to produce in their seminarians.

This is the real legacy of Bonhoeffer which is celebrated in this prayer, a legacy of costly discipleship which speaks of God in a god-less age, a legacy of prayer and hope at a time of 'well, whatever' culture, a belief that the Church ultimately belongs to Christ and calls men to their true nature by its life, rather than being simply a religious institution which risks being indifferent to whatever the state decides to do.

If we pray this prayer does Bonhoeffer's true legacy remain alive?

S tay simple and full of joy, the joy of the merciful, the joy of
brotherly love . . .
Refusing to look back, and joyful with infinite gratitude, never fear
   to rise to meet the dawn,
praising
blessing
and singing
Christ your Lord.

Brother Roger of Taizé

————◆◆————

I still have on my bookshelf the Rule of Taizé which I bought in
Taizé, in France, more than forty years ago. The story is that in the
early days of the community the Taizé brothers urged Brother Roger,
their Prior and Founder, to write a Rule of Life for the community.
They were a new community, finding their way, and needed shape
and direction. Presumably they had in mind the monastic rules of
other communities, especially that of St Benedict which shaped not
just the Benedictine Order but also the life of Europe for many
hundreds of years after. Brother Roger, however, was very reluctant,
for he did not see his community in quite the same way. This was a
community living the gospel life; it was not and should not develop
into an institution. Roger was well aware that so many religious communities began with a burst of life, much as, say, the Cistercians or
the Franciscans, but within a hundred years or less had become
hidebound institutions, full of rules rather than full of life.

   The Rule which he eventually wrote is a deeply luminous and
spiritual text, and I have referred back to it frequently during my life
and ministry. It does not tell the brothers when they should get up
in the morning or how they should dress or when they should eat. It
speaks of the basis of the spiritual life and derives so much of its
inspiration from the Gospels, especially the spirit of the Beatitudes
in Matthew 5. Instead of telling us when we should read the scriptures, the Rule says that we should allow our daily labour and rest to
be enlivened by the word of God. That is to say the word should be
always alive within us. Instead of telling us when we should be silent
and perhaps prescribing certain parts of each day or night as silent

times, the Rule says that we must keep within ourselves an interior silence in order to live in Christ. Then the Rule says,

Be penetrated by the spirit of the beatitudes, Joy, Simplicity and Mercy . . .

So this is the true rule of life. It comes as a surprise to find it is so simple. We are to be full of joy, simplicity and mercy. This is how Christians should be.

These words reflect that inspiration totally. Joy in life, simplicity of means in all things – remember how Christ 'ordered them to take nothing for their journey' – and mercy towards all whom we encounter. To meet those who live under this inspiration is to discover something entirely different, something from God.

O bright King of Heaven, surrounded by the starry hosts of angels, encompassed by the dark of mystery, which is the very effulgence of thy light: grant that we may glimpse thy beauty, and in that glimpse be cleansed, losing ourselves in thy glory.

R. E. C. ('Charlie') Browne

There is a great deal of misunderstanding in people's minds about mysticism and the mystical way. It is often thought to be for a few particular souls who may have special experiences of union with God while the rest of us struggle with prayer in a very ordinary and mundane way. What often causes difficulty is talk of 'the dark night of the soul', a phrase associated with St John of the Cross. People associate it with loss of faith or struggle to find God and so see it as a negative experience.

Reflection on this prayer by R. E. C. Browne, who was a much respected priest in Manchester after the Second World War, will reveal how the mystical way is neither negative nor particularly special. What it does is what all of the truly mystical writers do, that is, talk about light and darkness in the same breath. The prayer says that God is 'encompassed by the dark of mystery', but in the same sentence says that this is 'the very effulgence of thy light'. This mirrors exactly the language of earlier mystical writers. In his poem, 'The Night', Henry Vaughan wrote,

> There is in God (some say)
> A deep, but dazzling darkness;

And St John of the Cross talks about 'a ray of darkness', almost as if it were a ray of light. John of the Cross broaches this particular question directly and asks,

> Why, if it is a divine light . . . does one call it a dark night?

and goes on to compare the brightness of God's light with light which blinds the eye and causes the eye to register darkness rather than light.

> The more one looks at the brilliant sun, the more the sun darkens the faculty of sight.

So for St John and others in this tradition the dark night is due not to loss of light but to an excess of light, such an excess that the eye is blinded, much as looking directly at oncoming headlights causes dark patches to appear on the retina. So the mystical way is really the way which realizes that God is so bright, so intense that human sight cannot see God directly, which is itself a biblical insight.

The question remains that, if the mystical way is supposed to be for isolated and special people, what is a busy city priest like R. E. C. Browne doing writing about it in exactly the same way as John of the Cross and others? My own belief is that we all know something of the mystical way, for we are all aware of the uttermost glory of God, a glory that is so intense that it purifies and purges who we are. As St John says, which Browne's words echo,

> An inflow of God into the soul purges it of its habitual ignorances and imperfections.

O Christ our Lord,
  As in times past,
Not all the sick and suffering
Found their own way to your side,
But had to have their hands taken,
  or their bodies carried,
  or their names mentioned;
So we, confident of your goodness,
Bring others to you.

As in times past
You looked at the faith of friends
And let peace and healing be known,
Look on our faith,
Even our little faith,
And let your kingdom come.

We name before you
Those for whom pain is the greatest problem;
Who are remembered more for their distress
  than for their potential;
Who at night cry, 'I wish to God it were morning,'
And in the morning cry, 'I wish to God it were night.'
Bring healing, bring peace.

We name before you
Those whose problem is not physical;
Those who are haunted by the nightmares of their past
  or the spectres of their future,
Those whose minds are shackled to neuroses,
  depression and fears,
Who do not know what is wrong
And do not know what to pray . . .

Lord Jesus Christ, Lover of all
Bring healing, bring peace.

By John L. Bell © WGRG, Iona Community, G2 3DH

Clearly this prayer can go on and on, intercessions can be added at will, and I hope that you will use it as a springboard for the people you want to pray for; it can be used for all those for whom we wish to intercede.

I used it regularly on Friday evenings in Wells Cathedral. At Evensong on Fridays it has long been the custom to gather up the prayer cards which have been left in the cathedral by visitors during the previous week. These are placed at the candle stands which are found at various prayerful points around the cathedral, and visitors come, light a candle and say a prayer. They can write their prayers on cards and leave them pinned to a board so that others can use them, but on Friday the canon responsible for Evensong gathers the prayers together and uses as many as he can during the intercessions.

This is always the most moving time. People have come in with the most terrible burdens – children on drugs, husbands, wives or children dying, families split asunder – everything is there. Sometimes the prayers are written by children asking God for help for their parents; often they are from people who simply do not know what to do with their lives. Frequently those bereaved will return to the cathedral on the anniversary of their bereavement and leave a card asking the clergy to pray for the loved one they have lost. All of these are placed at the feet of Christ and, when I was at the cathedral, I used this prayer.

I used it because that cathedral community were, and still are, the friends of Christ and, although unknown as such, the friends of those who come. Just as friends brought their sick to Christ, carried on a bed or let down through a hole in the roof, so the community, in intention, does the same. They carry them to Christ.

To my mind this embodies the meaning of intercession. By praying for others we provide a leaning point so that these needs can be lifted more surely into God's presence. We can assist with the lifting. Moreover, this is what the family of the cathedral, or indeed any church, is for. It is there to pray for those who need prayer, who perhaps cannot pray for themselves, who are shy to come, nervous to come, who feel unworthy and far off. It can take their little cards, offered tentatively, flutteringly, and confidently bring them to God. In this way the cathedral family are friends for the world and for those in great need.

None of us needs a cathedral to do this. It can be done at home with others or without. What is important is that those with faith see themselves as intercessors, bringing closer to God the needs of those whose faith is so timid or fragile that they are afraid to do it themselves.

Even if that is all the Church does it is enough.

O Lord my God, most merciful, most secret, most present, most
constant, yet changing all things, never new and never old,
ever in action, yet ever quiet, creating, upholding and perfecting all,
who hath anything but thy gift? Or what can any man say when he
speaketh of thee? Yet have mercy upon us O Lord, that we may
speak unto thee, and praise thy name.

Jeremy Taylor, 1613–67 (based on a prayer of Augustine, 354–430)

This prayer embodies for me the known and unknown nature of
God. He is 'most secret' and yet also 'most present'. This prayer
comes before God, knowing of his existence but not able to say
anything about his existence, confident and yet silent. It is a prayer
which knows of God's mercy, of his redeeming and perfecting love,
but also of his quiet, his stillness. This is wonderful because it exhibits that quality of numbness before the presence of God which those
who really know him speak of.

If you read the diaries of Thomas Merton, particularly the diaries
of that period when he lived alone in his cinder block hermitage
outside of the monastery, you will find the same sense. He speaks of
the created order, of the birds that visit him, of the change in the
seasons, with the same awareness of God but also the same silence,
as if he had to hold his hand over his mouth to prevent himself from
speaking and yet could not do anything but speak. Too much prayer,
too much talk about God, is a torrent of words which in the end says
nothing, speaks to no one but the self who speaks.

In all prayer there has to be this sense of 'I must speak, but I
cannot speak,' 'I want to say something, but I cannot find even one
word which is adequate.' Without that, there is little sense of holiness, that it is in the end God to whom, about whom, we are speaking; without that, God is reduced to the level of another being, albeit,
of course, a very spiritual being, but another being much like us
nonetheless. Too much prayer dares too much and speaks too quickly.
We can only stumble towards him. We can only speak as he allows
and speaks in us.

Anything else is hubris.

O God, give us the discipline of attentiveness,
   attentiveness to each other and each other's needs,
attentiveness to the warp and woof of events and what they
   signify,
attentiveness to the created order about us, that we may
   hear its song.

Uphold with your grace this discipline in us Lord, so that we may
then catch the flash of love on another's face when we feared scorn,
the sudden glimpse of your kingdom in all the complexity of
human failure, and the flash of a kingfisher's wings on a dull day,
singing the song of newness and glory hidden deep in all things.

Melvyn Matthews

I was once the vicar of a conservative country parish. The people did
not want to change their ways of doing things, they disliked the new
services and much preferred the Book of Common Prayer, but they
worshipped faithfully week by week, full of prayer and dedication.
I used to say that they could sing Evensong with their eyes shut;
and they were very compassionate to the elderly and lonely in the
parish. One evening in Lent we were discussing some of the psalms,
and one person in the group, who was not somebody who welcomed
change and who 'kept the law' as it were, in her way of worship and
in her life, shared with the group an experience she had once had of
the love and presence of God. In this experience all things had been
shot through with grace and glory. It was a sort of mystical vision,
but not one in which God was separate from creation but one where
God was gloriously present in his creation. People and plants and
buildings were shot through with divine light.

That little sequence of events in a deeply but properly conservative English parish showed me how important the discipline of
attentiveness to things really is. The woman in question was a mus-
ician, but she was also studying science and astronomy. She read a
great deal and wrote some of the most beautiful poetry. She was
attentive to words and to things as well as to people. Then, suddenly,
she saw beyond the ordinary, she saw God at work.

My parishioner would not have seen beyond the ordinary had she not first observed the disciplines of her faith over a long time. Keeping this discipline of attentive love – which is one meaning of 'keeping the law' – meant that her heart and mind were prepared for the revelation of God. The interesting thing was that this revelation, when it came, was not something which told her to do something different, nor was it a revelation which led her to devote herself to missionary work or some extra church ministry, it enabled her to live more deeply what she had already been living. It sustained her daily life more surely. From that time she knew that whatever she touched was not ordinary, but that hidden within it was the real presence of God.

O God, help us when we listen to music or to another's voice, to listen for the silent music that is only heard when all other music stops. Open our inner ear to the music that enables other music to be made, to the tune which inhabits every tune, the song that the morning stars sang together when everything was made; and when we hear, give us grace to be silent and to praise your name.

Melvyn Matthews

I had to listen to a great deal of music in the cathedral where I worked. The services at the cathedral are almost always choral, and when the choirs are on holiday there are visiting choirs from America or other parts of the United Kingdom. After a number of years in a cathedral environment you come to know the regular repertoire quite well and can recognize differences of interpretation and standards of performance. The cathedral school is also a specialist music school, and so there are frequent concerts in the cathedral, with music to a very high standard.

My trouble was that I didn't like all of what I heard, and sometimes even what I liked was spoiled for me by the way in which it was performed. I used to feel that I should like more of it than I did, even all of it, but I lost that sentiment. I began to find that I was frequently listening for a certain quality of sound. I used to wonder what it was that I was listening for: should I not just enjoy the music or the performance and be glad that people can achieve so much? Was this not rather arrogant of me to try to find something else, even something that might just be in my own head rather than in the music itself?

But this inner listening has not gone away. I have come to think that what I am listening for is to do with poise and inner stillness. I hear it when the performer has listened to the music deeply enough to find some quality he or she wants to reproduce, something from elsewhere, and has found this because of his or her own stillness and poise. Then there is no rushing at the music, nor any treating of it casually, no rest or laziness either, but a poise which hears something from beyond.

In the novel *An Equal Music* by Vikram Seth, the string quartet which figures in the book set themselves to play a scale together whenever they rehearse. Playing this scale reminds them that however fraught their lives have been before they came together, they are, in fact, one.

What I am describing here is prayer. Prayer is attention to the music of God which he plays always. But it is not a music which can be heard on its own, neat, as it were, like neat whisky. God's music is constantly played in and through the music we make and is inside that music. Listening for it is prayer.

I can remember, one Christmas Midnight Mass in Wells Cathedral, hearing something of God's music being played. It came when the setting for the Mass was by Stravinsky, with long cold notes coming out of the air during the Gloria as if God were present – far off, but present, and calling to us that he was coming.

TWO EVENING PRAYERS

A bide with us, O Lord, for it is toward evening and the day is far spent; abide with us and with the whole Church. Abide with us in the evening of the day, in the evening of life, in the evening of the world. Abide with us in thy grace and mercy, in holy word and sacrament, in thy comfort and blessing. Abide with us in the night of distress and fear, in the night of doubt and temptation, in the night of bitter death when these shall overtake us. Abide with us and with all thy faithful ones, O Lord, in time and in eternity.

Lutheran Manual of Prayer

This is the Lutheran version of this lovely evening prayer. Anglicans will recognize that there is a shorter version in Common Worship Evening Prayer. I prefer this longer version, which has the richer imagery and deeper sense of our need.

It is full, of course, of biblical allusions. The word 'abide' is a particularly Johannine word and is full of the sense of deep participation in Christ which Jesus speaks of in that Gospel, the participation of the disciples in his life and of him in the life of the Father. So as we say this prayer we are drawn ever more deeply into the participative love of God and rest within the being of God, Father, Son and Holy Spirit.

What is of particular appeal to me is the reference in the first sentence to the story of the two disciples on the Emmaus road. These words, 'Abide with us for it is toward evening and the day is far spent', are the words the two disciples use to constrain the stranger they have met, and who has expounded the scriptures, to stay and eat with them (Luke 24.29 AV). As the stranger breaks the bread, they know that it is the Lord, and he then vanishes from their sight.

This story has always had particular meaning for me. A modern painting of the supper scene by the Welsh painter Ceri Richards, with Jesus breaking the bread and the two disciples falling back off their chairs in amazement, hangs in the chapel of the college I attended at Oxford. I used to love going in to stare at it when I was an undergraduate, and it figures on the cover of one of my books. But more importantly I can remember taking students to France to visit the monastery at Taizé in Burgundy and expounding this scene to them as we broke the bread together on the hillside there or in the minibus on the way home. It is a story which reminds me of the journey we are all making and of the way in which the Lord accompanies us on that journey, never forcing himself upon us, walking alongside, and in our puzzlement and difficulties over the faith simply saying, 'Well, look at it like this . . .' and showing us how things can be seen in another way, and so turning our hearts.

There are always moments when we are given the opportunity, as we travel, of seeing things differently and thereby being encouraged and supported in our faith. This is a prayer of thankfulness at the end of the day for such moments and a recognition of how they have brought us this far, to the place where we can lay down our hearts in peace.

G ive me this night, O Father, the peace of mind which is
truly rest.

Take from me

All envy of anyone else

All resentment for anything which has been withheld
from me

All bitterness against anyone who has hurt or wronged me

All anger against the apparent injustices of life

All foolish worry about the future

And all futile regret about the past.

Help me to be

At peace with myself

At peace with my fellow human beings

At peace with you.

So indeed may I lay myself down to rest in peace,
through Jesus Christ our Lord.

Source unknown

This prayer I often used at the end of Evensong in the cathedral
where I worked. My working days were busy, full of meetings
and conversations, full of the need to be aware of other people, of
colleagues, of worshippers, of the needs of the congregation, of the
school attached to the cathedral and which with others we cared for.
Like any busy person I moved from one set of concerns to another
very quickly and tried to prevent the worries of one affecting the
joys of another. So at the end of the day I was deeply grateful that
the Church gave me Evening Prayer to say. I was glad for the
very familiar and well worn pattern. The psalms for the day, read
slowly and antiphonally, a reading from the Hebrew scriptures, the
Magnificat, Mary's song of praise, then the New Testament reading
and the Nunc Dimittis, Simeon's words of thanksgiving; all this
regularity served to bring my disordered consciousness back into its
rightful order, my mental patterns were re-established as they needed
to be and I could see things in their right perspective.

This prayer acknowledges that I am a person of complicated emotions and thoughts, not all of them good. I suffer from envy, I am sometimes resentful, I am sometimes bitter with disappointment. I note injustices against me often well before I see them in action against others. I regret the past and long for fantasies I cannot and will not have. All of us are like this in some degree or another. This prayer with its honesty acknowledges all that at the end of the day and places it before God for his healing, for his correction and for his redeeming. It says: All that can and must be put aside, placed in God and grace poured over it all.

The first priest I worked with used to say that at the end of a long day we had to recognize that the Church we worked for was not ours, but God's. We had to give it back to him. This is the case with whatever work we undertake. Life is not ours, it is God's, and we have to return it to him at the end of each day with thankfulness, and allow him to correct, redeem and restore our work to us so that refreshed, and with a new sense of purpose, we can take it on in a new tomorrow.

THE FINAL ARRIVAL

O Christ of welcome and blessing, as we approach the heavenly city in which you dwell, make us glad with the shouts of greeting and encouragement from all those who have arrived ahead of us, and give us grace not just to return their cries, but to turn our heads to those who follow, maybe stumbling, behind us, and speak your words of welcome and blessing to them. So our gladness in the journey will be equal to our gladness in arrival.

Melvyn Matthews

The West Front of Wells Cathedral is justly celebrated for its ranks of medieval carvings, rows of angels, bishops, kings and characters from the scriptures; and carvings of incidents on one side from the Hebrew scriptures and on the other from the New Testament. At the top there is a carving of Christ, a modern portrayal by David Wynne, showing Christ with one hand uplifted in blessing and the other extended, an open hand of welcome. Immediately below him are the apostles, with Andrew, patron saint of the cathedral, in the centre and somewhat more to the fore than the others.

There have been several attempts to interpret this screen of figures, some more complex than others. At its simplest level the cathedral, like all European cathedrals from this period, was built to symbolize the heavenly Jerusalem, the city in which Christ dwells and to which we are all in pilgrimage. So the figures on the West Front at Wells are those who inhabit the heavenly city, who have reached the goal of life before us and are standing, looking out, waiting for the rest of us to come.

This symbolism came into its own in the Middle Ages when the Palm Sunday procession would come across the cathedral green as if this was the procession of Jesus and his disciples entering Jerusalem. The procession would be greeted by the sound of choirboys singing through the holes which can be seen between the figures at the lower level and, perhaps, by trumpets blowing from the holes at the topmost level. It would have been a colourful occasion.

Spiritually speaking this is all to remind us of our pilgrimage with Christ and his disciples to the heavenly city. Which it does, and gloriously. But those of us on the way have to recognize that Christ does not simply dwell at the end of the journey. He not only awaits us but also accompanies us, and he accompanies those who follow us, and those who follow them.

So my prayer is that however much we keep our eyes fixed on Jesus, the pioneer and perfecter of our journey, we also keep our eyes turned for those who come with us and behind us, and call to them in the dark and in the light, encouraging them and upholding them as they, with us, stumble towards the goal.